S0-BDO-597

WHAT IS WAR?

and

THE AGE OF DIVINE INTELLIGENCE

WHAT IS WAR?
Address of 1941

and

THE AGE OF
DIVINE INTELLIGENCE
Address of 1942

by

MARTHA WILCOX

The Bookmark
Santa Clarita, California

Copyright 2004 by Ann Beals

All rights reserved under the International
and Pan-American Copyright Convention

Library of Congress Number: 2004103881

Wilcox, Martha.
    What is war? : address of 1941 ; and, The age of divine
intelligence : address of 1942 / Martha Wilcox .
    P. cm.
    ISBN 0-930227-61-1

    1. Christian Science--Doctrines. 2. Christian
life-Christian Science authors. 3. Prayer. I. Title. II. Title:
Age of divine intelligence.
BX6945.W56 2004   289.5
                              QB104-200042

Published by
The Bookmark
Post Office Box 801143
Santa Clarita, California 91380

CONTENTS

3

WHAT IS WAR?
Association Address of 1941

43

THE AGE OF DIVINE INTELLIGENCE
Association Address of 1942

FOREWORD

In this book are two addresses that Martha Wilcox gave to her association of students at their annual meeting in Kansas City, Missouri. Mrs. Wilcox was a prominent teacher in the Christian Science movement from 1911 through 1948. Having been a school teacher before devoting her life to healing and teaching in the Christian Science Church, she could teach Christian Science in such a clear and simple way that her addresses have become classics.

Teachers occupied a very important role at that period in the Church. It was a great privilege to be chosen to go through the Normal Class of the Board of Education of The Mother Church, and become an authorized teacher of Christian Science. Those chosen to become teachers taught a class of thirty students each year. After two weeks of special instruction in Christian Science, the students then became members of the teacher's association. One day each year the teacher met with the association to give an address on Christian Science. Because of this, a great many association addresses were written during this early period in the Church.

The most outstanding teachers wrote papers that were profound insights unto the more advanced teaching of Christian Science. Association addresses were originally written exclusively for that teacher's association. Thus spiritually minded teachers wrote papers giving their deepest insights into the Science of God. During the prosperous years of the Church, they met a definite need for those students wanting a better understanding of Christian Science.

As the Church declined and the early teachers were no longer here, the dynamic teaching of the past slowly disappeared. Because the addresses of teachers were considered private papers intended only for their students, they were never published and most of them have been lost. But those addresses that have been saved, are becoming the lifeline connecting the dynamic years of the past with the present time when such teaching is no longer available. They are reviving the spiritual light that once burned so brightly. They can be compared to the letters that Peter, Paul and John wrote to the first Christian Churches. Although some of their early letters have probably been lost, those that remain continue to be an inspiration to Christianity. Even so, the association addresses that have come down to us are an inspiration today, and those by Mrs. Wilcox are among the finest.

The two addresses in this book, written during World War II, are as relevant to the present time as they were to students then. In her address "What Is War?" she goes beneath material warfare, defines "war" metaphysically, and how it must be overcome through prayer. Today the real battlefield seems to be mainly in the mental realm as the invisible threat of mind control poses as great a challenge as the visible threat of terrorism and war.

In the second address, she sees the coming of a spiritual age when war ends and humanity seeks a better way to find peace on earth. She could foresee the coming of an "age of divine intelligence." Slowly, but surely, the world seems to be wending its way into a future that transcends the old and learns the new. Her main theme – that all is mental and must be dealt with in the heart of our own consciousness – flows throughout both addresses. And this theme makes her writing timeless.

WHAT IS WAR?
Association Address of 1941

1. What Is War? ... 3

2. Malpractice ... 25

3. Healing by Means of
Christian Science Treatment ... 34

WHAT IS WAR?
Association Address of 1941

by

Martha Wilcox

1. WHAT IS WAR?

The purpose of today's lesson is to gain a truer and more comprehensive sense of the eventuality that we call war. Just what is war? According to the religious thought instructed in Christian Science, war is a warfare between Truth and error; a mental conflict between spiritual sense and material sense; a conflict between the flesh and the spirit which is spoken of in both the Bible and our textbook,Science and Health with Key to the Scriptures, by Mary Baker Eddy. Far too much is made of the seeming warfare, for we who are metaphysicians are proving each day that in the realm of infinite good there is not both good and evil, but good only. Hence there is no warfare.

War, according to the revelation of Christian Science, is mortal mind, or animal magnetism; and mortal mind, or animal magnetism, stands for all evil of whatever name or nature. It is the belief of life, substance and intelligence in matter; the belief of minds many and powers many. And the more we, as Christian Scientists, accept the suggestion that war is going on as a fact, the more we strengthen and perpetuate the belief of life in matter, the belief of minds many, and the more we are governed by mortal mind, or animal magnetism, instead of by the reality of being.

The belief of mortal mind, or animal magnetism, has no life or power or presence or being, therefore it cannot assert itself or

3

express itself as war. The belief of mortal mind, or animal magnetism, is not Mind, or conscious Life; therefore, it cannot be minds many — *it is not an entity filling space*. It has no presence or being; therefore, it cannot assert itself as a power or influence over people and cause discontent, disorder and murder. The whole claim of animal magnetism, or mortal mind, is without being, is without God in the world. War is purely the result of the belief that creation is material; but we through Christian Science know that all creation is spiritual, consisting of the sons and daughters of God, all having one Mind.

War seems to be a very great error, but we cannot properly invest error with gradations. No one error is greater or less than another error. All errors are mortal mind, or animal magnetism, and therefore unreal. All errors are unreal, and the war should not gain in seeming reality because of its seeming greatness. Mortal mind, or animal magnetism, in any form is nothing; and however great it may seem to be, it still is nothing. We should not make the mistake of believing that evils that confront us are great or small. In the demonstration of the one Mind, we find that error is neither great nor small. Our textbook teaches us that all errors are illusions, and an illusion is an unreal appearance.

The claim that error is personal in one instance and national or international in another, should not deceive us. God, Mind, Love, divine Principle, is infinite and All. The one Mind is conscious of everything that is true of men, and is conscious of everything that is true of nations, and whatever is not true of men and nations does not exist at all.

Where does this so-called war operate? Does it operate externally to us, or does it operate within us? All war is operating within what is ordinarily called human consciousness. It is not in any way external or remote from us. The war is entirely mental, no matter how much it may seem to the contrary, and it must be met in the mentality.

John records in Revelation, "There was war in heaven." Since there can be no war in heaven, harmony, the word 'heaven' is here unquestionably used to indicate a realm of thought; and sometimes there does seem to be a great conflict or war in what is ordinarily called human thought. Every problem that confronts us is wholly wrong thought, and all that can ever be done to the problem must be done in the realm of thought.

We cannot understand too well that whatever we take cognizance of and accept as a fact becomes a part of what is ordinarily called our human consciousness, and is reflected on our body or in our world. If we recognize and accept as a fact that there is war and dangers of war, we are not dealing with war scientifically, and the so-called war becomes our war or threatens to become our war. Those of us who read or listen to all the war news and think of war as actually taking place, are protected only because of mortal mind's belief that the war is apart and remote from us, instead of being a part of our human consciousness. Much is said about this war being the result of conflicting modes of thought — that barbarism is conflicting with Christianity; that totalitarianism is conflicting with democracy; that dictatorship is conflicting with individualism, and so on. But this so-called war is purely the result of a universal mass-mesmerism, an obsession — the so-called mortal mind's obsession that an increase of material good can be had only by external or extraneous additions of good. In other words, the expansion of so-called human good is by accretion, rather than by the unfoldment of spiritual ideas from within. This misconception of the expansion of material good is impelling Hitler, Stalin, Mussolini, and the Japanese to extend their control over territories and over the people of other nations. They are obsessed with the belief that there are no limits to the benefits of national expansion, and that no price is too great to pay for it. But in Christian Science, we understand that God made man, gave him presence, certainty, position, and man does not desire to get from somebody or some other nation, but draws from infinity.

The true and only method of expansion is revealed to us through our study of Christian Science. In *Science and Health* we read, "Christian Science presents unfoldment, not accretion; it manifests no material growth from molecule to mind, but an impartation of the divine Mind to man and the universe." Here we are taught that expansion of good is not by accretion, but results entirely from divine ideas within our consciousness. The only expansion is mental and spiritual. Spiritual expansion is heaven, harmony, and there are no limits to the benefits of spiritual expansion.

The situation called war is an extreme phase of mortal mind chemicalization, and we in Christian Science should have handled and taken care of this extreme chemicalization. Much of this eventuality is the result of work done in Christian Science, and the chemicalization produced should have been cared for by Christian Scientists. For many years through the activities of the Christian Science movement, Christ, or Truth, has been poured into universal human consciousness; and Christ, or Truth, has carried on its active work of redeeming human consciousness. But the material resistance of mortal mind to this active Christ, or Truth, has caused a great mental conflict throughout the world; and for want of a better name, we are calling this mental conflict war.

As an effect of this work done in Christian Science and under the pressure of this Christ, or Truth, that which purports to be the human mind with all its traditions, is being forced to a recognition of its own powerlessness and nothingness, and even its own self-destruction. This yielding of the so-called human mind to the divine Mind, is causing this great universal disturbance and chemicalization; and since mortal mind is both belief and believer, as one, it is its own self-destruction of persons and things. But this seeming self-destruction of mortal mind is not the destruction of anything actual, useful or valuable. It is the disappearance or dissolution of the false human concept of man as being a person and of things as being material. So long as this false human concept is entertained by us, it dulls our perception of that which is divinely true and just at hand.

Primarily we are not engaged in demonstrating over war, but as Christian Scientists we are primarily engaged in demonstrating the divine Principle, Love, in whose universe war does not exist. In demonstrating the divine Principle, Love, we as Christian Scientists may think we have failed miserably, because we have not as yet succeeded in bringing about conditions that are deemed desirable. This so-called war seems to involve so much of mortal mind and so many so-called mortals, that unless we are very alert, we may fail to vision the true character of success, or fail to recognize the present indications of success, because these indications do not tally up with our previous mortal mind conceptions of success.

I want to say emphatically that any apparent lack of results from our work in regard to this seeming conflict, is but the inability on the part of material sense to cognize what is taking place in this event called war. We, as Christian Scientists, should advance our thinking to a higher and more permanent mental and spiritual altitude, wherein we fully understand that our right thinking or our treatment has its origin and law in omnipotence, and that failure is impossible. Does this present war have a spiritual value for this epoch? All events and epochs are scientifically valueless unless they have a spiritual purpose. It is of little worth that wars and rumors of wars engage the printed page of thousands of newspapers; something more and something new is to be discovered and made practical. History shows that every epoch has its spiritual values, and happy are we who discern the spiritual values of this present time.

We closed last year's association meeting with this important statement: "This is the close of an era," and this morning allow me to make this statement: "We are now in the beginning of a new era." And this new era demands that each individual must see and hear with new distinctiveness and understanding. Jesus said, "Let him that readeth understand" and to the prophet Jeremiah, God said, "What seest thou?" If we read and see from the material sense of things, there will be "discord and dismay," but if we read and see from the spiritual vision, then there will be "Science and peace." We make our own choice.

7

The Coming of the Son of Man

Almost two thousand years ago, Jesus prophesied this present event, or this present war, but did not prophesy it as calamitous to those who "look up" above the sense testimony, or to those who "lift up their heads" — that is, lift up their thought to approximate Truth. True enough, he saw that all material, human concepts would vanish from the human mind; he saw that even "the powers of heaven shall be shaken" — that is, all mortal mind's established methods, customs, traditions, and values would be shaken and would give place to a new and higher order of things. (See Luke 21.)

In this prophecy, Jesus stated definitely and without question that the supremacy and reality of good would appear, and that evil would disappear from the world. According to Jesus' prophecy, this event is to be a triumph of and for Truth. Reality will be recognized and there will be the perception of the nothingness of nothing. Jesus added, "And then shall they see the Son of man coming in a cloud with power and great glory." The coming of the Son of man signifies that the demonstration of Christian Science is at hand. The Son of God is reality, or is all creation as it is; the Son of man is the human proof that all these realities are at hand. And the human proof or manifestation will approximate the perfection of these realities according to the degree that our individual thought individualizes divine Science.

The coming of the Son of man is not the coming of a person or the coming of something visible or spectacular — something outside of ourselves. No, the Son of man appears as higher, truer qualities of thought within ourselves. It is a great spiritual evaluation of the good that makes up our consciousness. We can in no way disconnect or disassociate the coming of the Son of man from God. The coming of the Son of man is God's presence appearing humanly, and is man and the universe seen and known according to our highest comprehension of their reality.

8

Referring to our present time, our textbook says, "As material knowledge diminishes and spiritual understanding increases, real objects will be apprehended mentally instead of materially." Jesus set forth clearly and definitely what should be our attitude of thought in these "latter days," and why we should have this attitude of thought. He said, "When these things begin to come to pass, then look up, and lift up your heads." Why? "For your redemption draweth nigh." Our redemption from what? Our redemption from the false concepts — the veil which has darkened man's vision, and which is done away in Christ. Christ, the truth about all things, is our Redeemer, and our redemption is at hand. We do not look at the destruction of something, but at the passing away of the false material concept of substance. This false concept of substance hides the omnipresence of man and the universe of reality. How readest thou? How seest thou? Instead of viewing the present time with dismay, Christian Scientists should assume their divine responsibilities. These may present themselves as human responsibilities; but since we know that they are divine and mental, they should be joyous responsibilities.

Each of us can and should assume the responsibility of handling the errors in his own thinking. We should do this as if we were the only one upon whom rested the responsibility for the correction to be made. In this way only do we work out our own salvation, and at the same time aid in working out the salvation of the world.

The New Age

At this present time we are leaving the era of a personal mind, and are being forced to rise to the demonstration of the divine Mind. The material resistance to this rise from a personal mind to the divine Mind is great. Those who depend upon personal mind alone can no longer demonstrate even ordinary sustenance. We have the example of how personal mind has planned peace and brought us war; the so-called mind of man has planned for abundance and yet millions are in want. Among the many spiritual values revealed to this age, there is none greater than the revelation that the intellect of man is not primarily human or personal, but is primarily divine intelligence, although as yet imperfectly disclosed. The Son of man — that is, divine intelligence — is coming to this age with great power. This is an incoming age of power and action, and dominion with works. The great need of the Christian Science movement today is not so much of the letter, but the power of Spirit — less teaching and talking, and more instantaneous, permanent healings.

We are leaving the 'talking age' for an incoming age of power and works. We all know far too well that the human personal mind has done much talking along every line, Christian Science included. There has been much talking in public affairs. There are talking congresses, talking legislatures, talking peace conferences, wordy diplomacy and so on and on. In business there are reports, sales propaganda, human opinions and the like. All talk! No doubt this talking age has fulfilled its purpose. The human mind has learned that talking is easier than seeking divine guidance; easier than action and good works. But man is also learning that talk does not produce actualities, and is not a substitute for actualities. The demand now is for dominion, power, action and works from us. To what extent are we preparing for these higher demands?

In reality what is taking place in this age, is what takes place in every Christian Science treatment, with the exception that what takes place in the individual consciousness through a treatment, is now taking place in cosmic or universal consciousness. And this that is taking place is the appearing of the reality of ever-present good, and the disappearing of all so-called evil. At this present time, we are witnessing the ascendancy and supremacy of good, and the powerlessness, the nothingness and self-destruction of evil, even though the sense testimony is to the contrary. We would be mightily discouraged if we did not understand this great and vital truth.

Every event in so-called human history has been for the triumph of Truth. This is clearly seen in what frequently appears as a war or conflict, but what, in its actuality, is the demonstration of the omnipotence and omnipresence of good, and the powerlessness and nothingness of evil. We read in our textbook, "The manifestations of evil, which counterfeit divine justice, are called in the Scriptures, 'The anger of the Lord.' In reality, they show the self-destruction of error or matter and point to matter's opposite, the strength and permanency of Spirit. Christian Science brings to light Truth and its supremacy, universal harmony, the entireness of God, good, and the nothingness of evil." It also says, "The breaking up of material beliefs may seem to be famine and pestilence, want and woe, sin, sickness, and death, which assume new phases until their nothingness appears. These disturbances will continue until the end of error, when all discord will be swallowed up in spiritual Truth."

The end of any error will come to us individually when the error becomes extinct within our human consciousness. When we give a Christian Science treatment, there should be the extinction of some particular error, and the extinction should be permanent. Yes, wars — which are purely error — will continue until the cause of the war is exposed and vanquished, made extinct in human consciousness.

Moral Chemicalization

Our textbook states, "Mortal error will vanish in a moral chemicalization." Moral chemicalization is taking place at this time and the errors of mortal thought are vanishing from human consciousness. In the coming age, human consciousness will be characterized by moral excellence — that is, our manners, customs, habits, conduct and ways of life, pertaining to the action of men and nations, will spring from man's natural sense of rightness and propriety. We all understand that man's natural sense has its source in divine Principle, Love; therefore man's natural sense will show forth the qualities of graciousness and mercy with justice to all.

Since mortal error is vanishing in a moral chemicalization, it is fitting that we understand the nature and character of chemicalization and what produces it. In *Science and Health*, Mrs. Eddy tells us, "What I term *chemicalization* is the upheaval produced when immortal Truth is destroying erroneous mortal belief." According to this definition, our present so-called war is a chemicalization or an upheaval produced by immortal Truth destroying erroneous mortal beliefs. And what an upheaval seems to be taking place "as truth urges upon mortals its resisted claims!" There would be no chemicalization or upheaval at this time, were it not that the claims of truth are being resisted to the hilt by mortal mind.

The word 'chemicalization' is usually associated with a process of fermentation, but in Christian Science chemicalization is purely mental — that is, it is taking place wholly within what is ordinarily called the human consciousness. Mrs. Eddy says, "Mental chemicalization follows the explanation of Truth, and a higher basis is thus won." She also says, "Mental chemicalization brings sin and sickness to the surface, forcing impurities to pass away." Again she says, "By chemicalization I mean the process which mortal mind and body undergo in the change of belief from a material to a spiritual basis." From these definitions we readily see that chemicalization is occasioned whenever we change our erroneous human concept of persons and things to a spiritual and true concept of persons and things. Some may ask, Is such chemicalization necessary? It will take place just so long as there seems to be both Truth and error, both good and evil in our consciousness. Chemicalization is the natural process we undergo in our change from belief to Truth, or it is the transformation of the human to the divine. But this change, or transformation, should be effected without pain or aggravation to either mind or body. Mrs. Eddy says, "This fermentation . . . should be as painless to man as to a fluid." And chemicalization would be painless, if it were not for the seeming material resistance to Truth in our consciousness.

Chemicalization, produced by the action of absolute Truth

when absolute Truth is poured into human consciousness, is a belief which cannot be ignored. It needs much more consideration than most workers in Christian Science give it. Many Christian Scientists in their practice work and in their work concerning the world's problems, fail to recognize the need of handling the claims of harmful chemicalization. Mrs. Eddy plainly indicates that chemicalization should be dealt with through the realization that divine Love expressed is the only presence, power, or consciousness.

In the process of the appearing of real civilization, the old civilization chemicalized, and a new and higher civilization appeared. Real civilization has never failed, but the pretense has failed miserably. Nevertheless even the mere pretense of civilization is better than barbarism. Without civilization in some degree, we would have no Christianity and no Christian Science.

Someone may ask, Is this chemicalization which is brought about by the revelation and demonstration of Christian Science so severe that it is destroying civilization, rather than redeeming it? Surely, we do not believe that the practical demonstration of Christian Science could produce harmful chemicalization; rather should we take the attitude that we have the ability to care for any chemicalization that seems to be produced through the demonstration of Christian Science. And if in our work, our thought takes on something of the grandeur of God, this true thought, or Truth, will take care of any situation that may arise.

God Governs the Universe

Civilization will not be destroyed; government will not be destroyed; and the reason they will not be destroyed, but appear better unto their perfection, is because they are already perfect and established in the Mind which is God.

True civilization and true government cannot be imposed upon by any individual. Civilization and government are ideas of Mind, and must eventually spring from within. Science teaches that man, self-governed by divine Principle, is ideal government. This government of Mind is neither capitalistic nor communistic, but is exclusively and inclusively Christian. This real government seems quite remote if we look to the testimony of the senses; but looking within, each one of us may establish divine government, and each one of us may exemplify divine government, and in so doing we hasten divine government for all mankind. Only Christian Scientists understand the import of these days. With our pure thought, we are looking through and beyond the mists of war, which are merely an appearance of evil, and we are glimpsing war's underlying reality — a new and true civilization, a new and divine government.

Omnipotent, omniscient, omnipresent God governs the universe harmoniously and eternally, and in this government there are no secret organizations and no fifth columnists that can govern or influence men and nations erroneously. Reason and logic show us conclusively that what appears as a human being with life and intelligence in and of himself, is none other than Mind's presence. Divine Mind has unfolded Himself out into this particular so-called personality. All there is to any personality, or all there is to anything this personality may seem to be or to do, is divine Mind, Himself, being and doing it. Therefore, man cannot be governed or influenced by anything but the divine Mind.

Christian Scientists have power over evil beliefs because the Christ, or Truth, that they individualize, is power. Thinking rightly about the war is greater than the war. Which is greater, your understanding or the war? Your understanding is God with you, while war is error, therefore nothing. We Christian Scientists, as exponents of Truth, have sufficient understanding to protect those at the head of our government, to protect our nation and to protect all nations. We should clearly discern that any nation and all nations, our government and all governments, reflect wisdom and intelligence, and cannot be influenced erroneously.

Since we embrace our civilization, our government and our

universe in our thought, we should know that our true thought, or Truth, governs all harmoniously. Let us rid our thought of hate, malice and anger. Let us rid our thought of the desire to get even with somebody or some nation. Let us rid our thought of rivalry and contention, and maintain a clearly defined mental position based on Truth.

Such realization of Truth is the law of annihilation to the belief of destruction, devastation and death. Such realization will do something to the war, and will eventually destroy all sense of or belief in war. When we take the mental position that God is all, then man in His image and likeness cannot be an instrument through which hypnotism, suggestion and deception can work. A position that God is all, is a law of annihilation to the belief of fear, contention, or animal magnetism of whatever nature. When we take the mental position that God and man is one being, this basic truth is a law of education, enlightenment, discernment of the divine presence, expressed as the idea of infinite Love. "Love is the liberator."

Preparedness and Defense

Among students of Christian Science there has arisen the question whether material preparedness and defense are necessary, or whether spiritual preparedness and defense alone are sufficient. Now, in order that spiritual preparedness and defense may be equal to the emergency at hand, our understanding must be the understanding to demonstrate God's allness, then there is no need for material preparedness and defense. But so long as we are taking our human footsteps, which are indispensable, we do need intelligent material preparedness and defense. It seems that we, in our present growth, are in a stage of semi-metaphysics wherein "arguments are based on the false testimony of the material senses as well as on the facts of Mind." But surely no one will underestimate the value of spiritual preparedness and defense, without which no victory is really won. There is nothing soft or weak or effeminate about spiritual preparedness and defense. Spiritual preparedness and defense are the power of divine Love, and are as keen as a blade. It takes strength of character and discipline of thought and great courage for us to become spiritually prepared to the extent that we have an adequate defense for every emergency. But any degree of spiritual preparedness, however small, is of utmost value.

Bible history shows us that no matter how great the material preparedness and defense of armies, it is only when spiritual power enters into the arena that victory is won. Why is this so? Because the operations of armies are based on material observations and sense testimony, on fear, hate, pride, and it is only when the spiritual element enters in that victory for right is won.

Take for example the armies of Abram. They were considered an adequate defense in that day. They moved as a tower of strength in their preparedness of horsemen and chariots, spears and swords in great array. But even these great warriors fell back before the oncoming hordes of the enemy, whose fiendish yells of victory were heard above the cries of defeat of Abram's armies. During this long night of defeat and terror, Abram, the one righteous man, watched for the coming of Melchizedek, the priest of the most high God. Melchizedek came with the coming of the morning, but not with arms and great numbers of men. He came with only a few attendants. Yet the armies arrayed against Abram saw this vision of omnipotence — this coming of Melchizedek — as a great army advancing swiftly upon them. They saw their own fears personified and fell back upon their own swords and were self-destroyed. Then Abram and his armies knew that God — the power of right Mind — was the spiritual defense of His people, their strong deliverer.

Again we would say that the armies of Israel, arrayed as they were against the Philistines, were great armies, both in size and ability; but the armies of Israel were not adequate for victory over the Philistines. The victory came when David challenged

Goliath saying, "Thou comest to me with a sword, and with a spear, and with a shield: but I come to thee in the name of the Lord of hosts, the God of the armies of Israel, whom thou hast defied. And all this assembly shall know that the Lord saveth not with the sword and spear: for the battle is the Lord's, and he will give you into our hands."

Both Abram and David had within themselves spiritual preparedness. They had gained this spiritual preparedness and power which was their strong defense through many trying experiences. Abram and David had within themselves clearly defined mental positions, and these mental positions were based on spiritual understanding, not on sense testimony, newspaper reports, radio announcements and other means. When Abram and David were confronted with overwhelming problems, they had no question or doubt as to the outcome of the situation because their mental position was the infinitude and allness of God.

Correcting the Belief in War

Some may ask, Should we never read or listen to the war news? To ignore the war news would not help in any way to overcome the belief in war. But to read all the war news and listen to all the radio broadcasts and saturate our mentalities with the horrors of war, only to have these reflected on our bodies, in our homes and business conditions, does not in any way help us or in any way correct the belief in war. If we do read and listen, it should be for the purpose of handling the error intelligently. Our recognition of man's oneness with God should be a law to the seeming situation. We should not be terrorized by what we hear, but we should deny it, and handle it, and never accept it as fact. Like Abram and David, our thought should be clearly defined as to the facts in the case.

The mental position of each individual student of Christian Science should be clearly defined when it comes to the social-economic revolutions that confront our world today, and especially when it comes to war. We should base our thinking on the allness of God, and we should be persistent and insistent in establishing a mental position based on Truth. When our mental positions concerning the experiences that seem to be taking place humanly are based on divine facts, they are always accompanied with divine power. The time has come when spiritual Truth must be the guide to practical life. We as Christian Scientists must seek, accept and fulfill the guidance of spiritual power, which is always above the concepts of the human mind.

As working Christian Scientists, we say that the understanding of Christian Science is equal to every difficulty, whether the difficulty is great or small. These are days of seeming great difficulties and great tribulation, and these are wholly mental and must be met in the mentality. Our demonstrations of the divine facts at hand will depend entirely upon the mental position we maintain; and the results will be in the exact proportion that our thought is based either on sense testimony or on the Science of Mind.

All power is in the right thought or in the divine idea that we individually entertain. This is the only power in the universe. Thinking rightly, or establishing the fact about any situation, governs and controls aright the human concept. The power of right thought is in the thinking of it, or in the realization of it. Our understanding is God with us, and is the only power with which we demonstrate. We often hear it said that God governs the war. Let us remember that God is not something separate or remote from man, so we cannot leave all the responsibility of the war to a remote power. What we individually know of Truth is power, and is God in action.

To sense, the war is appalling, but the apathy and indifference and inactive attitude of thought towards the war among the Christian Scientists, is far more appalling. To sew and to knit and to make garments is a commendable thing, but it is never a substitute for the power of Truth, or true thought, within the individual consciousness, which is most vital at this time. Day by day, we should know that nothing unlike good is taking place. When we read or cognize that our liberty is being threatened by the dominating powers of autocracy, we can even take care of that, because our idea of what is true, or the true idea which we individually entertain, is Principle, and as we establish our thought on the side of Principle, this Principle is the law that governs and cares for the universe.

There seem to be two sides to every question — both belief — but our treatment will meet the claim of evil that threatens to overcome the better side or the better belief. As we know there is but one power, one thought, one side, then what seems to be the better side or the better belief will prevail. Principle and its action is law. Principle and its action is the law to man, that he shall be a state of harmony instead of a state of discord; that he shall be a state of liberty instead of a state of bondage.

In regard to our country, we need to know that "the government shall be upon his shoulder." Then we can slip out from under the burden and let Truth unfold. We manage to do a lot of things when once we sense the power of right thought, and realize that the right ideas which we entertain are one with Principle and are law to any situation. We should keep uppermost in our consciousness that God — Mind — is infinite, all power, all action; and then we are able, as Mrs. Eddy says, "to mightily rebuke a single doubt of the ever-present power of divine Spirit to control all the conditions of man and the universe."

To waken Christian Scientists throughout the world to a recognition of pure metaphysics and to a right sense of affirmation and denial, is one of the tasks that lies before us, and this awakening comes only through the demonstration of Love. Christian Scientists in every nation must awaken to the necessity of denying their own faults and the faults of their own nation, and these seeming faults must be denied until they are extinguished from consciousness. In every Christian Science treatment the only adequate denial is the absolute nothingness of any phase of evil.

19

Handling Fear

The international outlook presents a few great nations glorifying war and the rest of the nations fearing war. The errors are national pride and national fear; thus we are apt to deceive ourselves when it comes to these errors and merely handle national pride. The fear of nations is very great (if we admit any error to be great) and we should handle this claim of fear. Let us remember that the reality and individuality of every nation, as well as the reality and individuality of every man, is forever intact in God and is eternal. The reality and individuality of a nation cannot be lost, but is found in the harmony of its infinite Principle — Love.

The desire to wipe a certain nation off the map, or to feel great disapproval of any person or group of persons, is not a correct scientific attitude for any Christian Scientist to take. To make any error, however great, a personal error, is not the way to prove its nothingness. Our work as Christian Scientists is to prove the powerlessness and nothingness of erroneous thought, wherever it is seen or whatever its form, through our own correct mental position of God's allness. As we realize that we are of the Spirit of God, we can control every situation; but in Christian Science we must be scientific in our thinking, or we shall make no demonstrations. As Christian Scientists, we have a responsibility far greater than adherents of other religions, because the truth about all men and nations has been revealed to us.

Our textbook, when speaking of the power of God in healing both mind and body, says, "The tree is typical of man's divine Principle, which is equal to every emergency, offering full salvation from sin, sickness, and death." And St. John the Revelator writes, "And the leaves of the tree were for the healing of the nations." The leaves of the tree stand for pure metaphysics, and any error pertaining to man or nations that is cognized by pure metaphysics, comes under their all-powerful healing influence.

It is quite natural that each one of us should be vitally concerned about our own country, the United States, and about our own boys; and yet we experience the protective power and healing influence of pure metaphysics in the proportion that we maintain the fact that divine Mind is in operation as all consciousness. God, Mind, is not only in operation as the consciousness of Christian Scientists and the consciousness of our country and our boys; but God, Mind, is in operation as the consciousness of the whole world. In other words, the one infinite consciousness is not exclusively aware of me as a Christian Scientist, and aware of my country and my boy, however much these may engage my attention. If I desire protection for myself or my country or my boy by means of divine Science, my protection is in the exact proportion that God — my Mind — knows no distinction of nations or persons or boys. As I understand and maintain that God — my Mind — is the only substance, presence, power and law to that which constitutes my consciousness humanly as nation, country or boy, this realization not only protects me and my country and my boy, but protects all men and all nations.

Last October I read a personal letter written by a young Canadian soldier, who had been through the battle in France before France capitulated and also the evacuation from Dunkirk. He was at the time acting as a pilot in the Royal Air Force in England. The letter was written to his Sunday School teacher and practitioner, who had spent much time with him in preparing his thought for the many problems that might confront him. This young man quite thoroughly understood the distinction between man and the illusion that appeared as fighting mortals. The practitioner had made it especially clear to the young man concerning the allness and omnipotence of God, and how this omnipotence and omnipresence of God was the substance and the wholeness of every human being. She told him that the omnipresence of God could not be pierced by a bullet. This statement of Truth appealed to the youth so much that he wrote it out and placed it on the control panel of his plane, so

21

that it was right before him. Arrangements were made that if anything should happen to this boy, a cable was to be sent to the practitioner. One day a Nazi bomber shot down his plane and he fell to the earth, but even while falling the thought was with him that omnipresence was the substance and the wholeness of everything. They picked him up, took him to the hospital, and then cabled the practitioner.

The young pilot seemed terribly mangled, and the next morning his friends went to the hospital expecting to find him dead, but instead he was alive, with no broken bones. The practitioner had proved that the omnipresence of conscious Life is the substance and the wholeness that constitutes man. Within a week the youth was back piloting another plane! The practitioner understood pure metaphysics, and her mental position of God's allness was an adequate defense. She neither affirmed nor denied the illusion — the mere appearance called personal man — but she realized that in the omnipresence of God, "There is neither Jew nor Greek, there is neither bond nor free . . . for [we] are all one in Christ."

A New Perspective

Mortals may say, What is the remedy for the multitudinous problems of the world? We know that men evolve and formulate wise laws and just agreements, which to some extent relieve the world's troubles; but mankind is absolutely powerless to change the human heart from which every form of evil springs. Christ, Truth, Love, alone can do this.

The hope of the world lies in a higher power than human greatness and might. Human wisdom and ability cannot save the world in the perilous hour, but deliverance will come from the Lord who made heaven and earth. And let us remember that 'the Lord' is the right idea or true consciousness which we entertain concerning all things. The thinking of right thoughts or spiritual ideas is the only power in the universe.

22

We should not be dismayed at man's apparent helplessness. These days are teaching us, universally, the need of divine help. The call of this hour is that man shall return to God, or Truth, because Truth is the only remedy for human ills, and as Christian Scientists we should be giving more attention to spiritual values and moral excellence than ever before. The supreme need in the world today is for a religion that will lead the people to almighty God and unchangeable Truth, and this religion is the Science of Mind, or Christian Science. The hope of the world is in Christian Science. The world is desperately in need of a new perspective — in need of an interpreter and an interpretation — and it is coming today into our midst. "What seest thou?" The coming of the Son of man — even the demonstration of divine Science in our midst. Everything that we now know humanly will be understood in its reality, and will be seen visibly, and thus known tangibly in its divinity.

Are we, with our pure thought, looking through and beyond the mists — the mere appearances of evil? And are we beholding these appearances as the hidden existence of good? The infinity of good is discernible in men and nations, since men and nations exist as the manifestation of infinity.

Since our own Mind is the one Mind, it must be pure Science, and pure Science is the only effective power in healing the false testimony that confronts the world today. When we understand the fact concerning men and nations, and remove our thought from the sense testimony, this fact of men and nations is enlightening and comforting and reassuring. Let us keep uppermost in our thought that infinite consciousness is infinitely conscious of all His own. "The Lord hath been mindful of us," we read in Psalms. There is no limit to the good we can do when once we refuse to accept the limitations which so-called mortal mind would impose upon us. To become conscious of the world as God is conscious of it, is to overcome the world as Jesus did — that is, to overcome the false human concept of the world. The more we cognize the power we possess, as right thought or divine idea, and exercise this power

23

in a God-like manner, the more we observe the effect of our work. The result is apparent not only to ourselves, but is apparent to all mankind.

Preparing for the New Age

Perhaps the most important truth of all for us to understand today, is that God has chosen us to live in these very years. Just as much as it was in divine order that Jesus appeared to humanity in his age, and that Mary Baker Eddy appeared to humanity in her age. Out of the billions of persons seemingly born to other ages, we have been chosen to live in this present time, and be present at the christening of a new age.

The world is so confused that unless we recognize that God has chosen us, and that we are in divine order, we will fail to prepare ourselves for the coming of the Son of man, which is the Son of God, fail to prepare ourselves for the spiritual riches that are appearing. Each of us should prepare himself mentally and spiritually. We do not need to bother about anything else. Each one of us should change himself in order to be prepared for the new age.

We need not try to change God, and it is useless for us to try to turn new conditions back into old conditions. Our only problem today is to prepare ourselves to fit into the new conditions of a new world, which is the coming of the Son of man or the demonstration of divine Science.

Old things and old conditions are passing away. "Behold I make all things new." The world of mortals is chaotic; it is the breaking up of old beliefs. We see the sign of the coming of the Son of man in all the fluctuations and changes that are taking place today. We are not afraid, but rather do we rejoice that the long night of materialism is fading and the dawn of a new spiritual day is at hand.

2. MALPRACTICE

The Correct Way to Handle This Claim

A great many things have been said in the past, and many things are being said now, about malpractice, which do not tend to clear the thought of Christian Scientists concerning the claim of malpractice. Much time and energy have been worse than wasted on the part of earnest students in the endeavor to handle this particular error. There is a correct way to handle the claim of malpractice, and we should understand the correct way, and then follow it effectually.

There are two divergent views concerning what is known as mental malpractice. On the one hand, we often find persons looking here and there trying to discover some hidden thing, which they at once label malpractice. On the other hand, we find students prone to ignore the claim of malpractice altogether, when they should recognize it and deal with it.

Mrs. Eddy's definition of mental malpractice is most enlightening and deserves far more attention than we usually give it. In *Miscellaneous Writings* she says, "Mental malpractice is a bland denial of Truth, and is the antipode of Christian Science." In other words, mental malpractice is a state of mind which is the exact opposite of Truth, or the exact opposite of divine Mind. Now, the exact opposite of divine Mind is the so-called mortal mind, therefore mortal mind is all malpractice. This does not mean that all human beings are intentionally malpractitioners; but the majority of human beings, believing in matter instead of understanding Spirit, do unconsciously malpractice upon themselves and others much of the time.

Mrs. Eddy set forth two phases of mortal mind or mental malpractice. First, the bland or soothing denial of Truth. These bland or soothing modes of mortal mind are never stimulating, rather

25

do they put us at ease in matter. They put us in a state of non-resistance to the beliefs of mortal mind. These bland and soothing modes of mortal thought impose upon us the mental qualities of indifference, lethargy, apathy, mental laziness, inaction — all of which we may be quite unconscious of. They impose upon us the limitations of capacity, ability, endurance — modes of thought which are the very opposite of man's God-given dominion.

Let us illustrate how mortal mind with its bland or soothing denials of Truth, all unconsciously takes possession of us and puts us to sleep. There was a student of Christian Science who had severe business reverses. He was nearing his sixtieth year, and mortal mind through its bland and soothing suggestion had definitely convinced this man that he was shelved for the rest of his life. Mortal mind said there was no position for a man sixty years of age; there was no money to start a new business with; conditions were never so unfavorable; he could not cope with the new ways of doing business. Mortal mind told him it was just impossible for him to again achieve success, and there was nothing for him but to retire from active life and apply for an old age pension. Now, such bland denials of Truth did not in any way stimulate this student, but instead they lulled him to sleep. Here was a man in the prime of life, thoroughly mesmerized into a state of non-resistance to the beliefs of mortal mind.

But his wife recognized these modes of mortal mind thought as the exact opposite of the divine Mind, or the true expansive modes of thought. She took the mental position that man is never separated from God, good, and finally through Christian Science the truth prevailed. This man entered upon an entirely new line of work, something quite simple and inexpensive, but something that developed into a very active and remunerative business. He is happy now in proving that any idea, no matter how small to mortal belief, is expansive and infinite when seen from the standpoint of divine Spirit.

The second phase of mortal mind or mental malpractice

which Mrs. Eddy sets forth is a phase that appears to be more aggressive, more intentional, or maliciously directed. It seems that there are persons who would harm us — morally, physically, or spiritually — but any such appearance should always be classified as belief, and never as an actuality. Malicious mental malpractice, so-called, is not so much directed thought (since there is no personal mind) as it is universal belief — the universal belief that there are minds many and some very wicked minds.

Mrs. Eddy never, in any of her writings, gives power or reality to mental malpractice, but keeps it entirely in the realm of belief. In *Miscellaneous Writings*, she says, "Its claim to power is in proportion to the faith in evil, and consequently to the lack of faith in good. Such false faith finds no place in, and receives no aid from, the Principle or the rules of Christian Science; for it denies . . . that God, good, has all power." She adds in substance that if one retains his faith in mortal mind and personal evil, he is on the "broad road to destruction."

Of course, it would be absurd for Christian Scientists or any other Christian to ignore the apparent wickedness of mortal mind, and especially the wickedness that is malicious. We are admonished in our textbook to deny malicious malpractice. If we believe that we are the object of some evil thought, mentally directed, we should handle this belief and never admit it as anything other than belief. We should handle the belief that there is a personal wicked mind, and handle it entirely within our own thought, and handle it with the actual understanding that God, good, is the only Mind. Only in this way do sin and malpractice become extinct in human consciousness.

War is the apparent wickedness of mortal mind; but when "we know that the nothingness of error is in proportion to its wickedness," and "the greatest wrong is but a supposititious opposite of the highest right," as we are told in our textbook, then we shall understand that war and all the seeming activities of so-called mental malpractice, are in the realm of belief only.

27

Handling Material Resistance to Truth

Because of the seeming prevalent activity of so-called mortal mind, at this time expressing itself in calamity, accident, loss and destruction, we should handle malpractice daily. We do not handle it as personal, but we do handle it as opposition or material resistance within the human consciousness to Truth.

What do I mean by handling material resistance within the human consciousness? Let me illustrate: A Christian Science student called me some time ago and asked for help for herself. She was greatly disturbed because her husband had been drinking heavily. He was not a Christian Scientist. I said to her, "Let us handle material resistance to Truth within your own consciousness." She said, "Why, Mrs. Wilcox, what do you mean by that? I do not resist Truth." I said, "You know the truth, and the truth is that someone who appears to you as a human being, mesmerized by sin, is in reality the son of God and divine in being. Now the carnal or mortal mind within your consciousness resists this truth, or contends against this truth, by picturing itself as a personal man mesmerized by the drink habit. The truth or fact in your consciousness — that man is God's presence — is resisted by the misconception of man — that he is a personal, mortal, sinning man."

Students, let us handle — that is, make nothing of — mortal mind beliefs and mental malpractice. Let us see the nothingness of these bland or aggressive denials of Truth within human consciousness. Let us handle them with ever increasing intelligence and effectiveness, but at the same time let us be wise in dealing with the beliefs of mental malpractice. In the face of the fact that our books abound in the clear explanation of good, and the allness of the Mind that is Love — the Love that thinketh no evil — yet we find Christian Scientists speaking of evil as if it were actually occurring, and we find them constantly contending with what they call malpractice, just as if it were a reality.

It is incorrect, not to say foolish, for a Christian Scientist to imagine all sorts of evil, and then to proceed to work against the creations of his own imagination. Evil, or error, or belief is not something, but is always nothing. Evil, or error, or belief is not something that one fights or rejects or ejects. If we have something that we must reject or struggle to eject, we are making a reality of it, and we are adding more difficulties to what originally appeared to require our attention.

Where does mental malpractice operate? Mental malpractice claims to operate or exert itself only in its own realm of belief. If we claim divine being and accept no personal sense of ourselves — or in the measure that we do this — we are exempt from any consensus of human opinions or any specific effort of mortal mind to injure us or make us ill.

It is surprising to meet student practitioners of long standing who believe that they are suffering for "righteousness' sake." Such an attitude of thought is an open door for all kinds of suggestions. The one who believes that he is attacked because he is a Christian Scientist, needs to handle malpractice not as something directed toward him, but he needs to handle his own mesmeric belief of malpractice. The significant thing about this particular claim — that one suffers because he is a Christian Scientist — is that the Christian Scientist who is suffering fails to see that he should handle his own mesmeric belief in malpractice. His own mesmeric belief is rarely ever discernible to the Christian Scientist who imagines that he is subject to malpractice. It is not humanly reasonable to suppose that here and there are certain Christian Scientists being selected by malpractice to be the victims for its administrations. Let us more and more take our thought from malpractice as an entity doing something, and understand it as false mesmeric belief in individual consciousness, or understand it as resistance of mortal mind to the truth in individual consciousness.

If, in any instance, we have seemed to pass through the fire and walk through the waves, we can even now recognize the unreality of all such dreams. If we, as Christian Scientists, had always striven to demonstrate the presence of Mind, instead of merely seeking to bring about some human desire, there would have been no waves and no fire for us to pass through. But if we were not wise enough to avoid the waves or the fire, we may rejoice in a more active awakening through which we are now undeceived.

Man's Oneness with God

It is necessary to have within ourselves a clearly defined mental position concerning our oneness with Life, Truth, and Love; otherwise our mentality is a constant denial of what we actually are, or is a constant malpractice upon ourselves. The distinctive feature of Mrs. Eddy's work in behalf of humanity is seen in her clear perception of what man is and his oneness with God.

Prior to the discovery of the Science of Mind, the trend of all religious teaching was to relegate man to the realm of inferiority and sin. The human race accepted the testimony of the senses as real, believing the personal man to be man. And in religion human beings could hardly do otherwise than believe that they were sinners and inferior to God. Hence in belief, the malicious malpractice upon one's self was established in religion.

The tendency of the whole Christian Science movement, at this present time, is to fall back to old theology, and think of man according to the testimony of the senses, as a sinner and desperately wicked. This attitude of thought harms the individual who is thinking it, more than it harms anyone else. It is a constant malpractice upon man. There should be a definite mental stand against this tendency by Christian Scientists. We, as exponents of Christian Science, should maintain the theology of Jesus, which was "perfect God and perfect man, — as the basis of thought and demonstration."

Too often, Christian Scientists keep themselves and others in an intermediate realm, wherein they are material mortals now, but through a process of salvation will sometime become immortal. They keep themselves in a realm wherein they affirm the truth and merely resist the error, instead of *extinguishing* it. This is particularly true when it comes to the question as to whether we are mortals now or immortals now. We should detect and reject this subtle malpractice that would ever keep us believing that we are mortal and sinful now, and that eventually we are to be made immortal and sinless by a process of salvation.

Students, is our mental position one of truth about ourselves and others or is it one of malpractice? Do we have within ourselves a mental position of clearly defined Truth, and are we thinking and living from this position? If we think that we are a sinning mortal and that others are sinning mortals, this thought is a sin against the Holy Ghost, against divine Science. If we think such thoughts, we are mental malpractitioners.

What is our state of mind this instant? Is it Truth or is it malpractice — a denial of Truth? Are we this instant man or are we the false concept of man? Are we this instant spiritual or material? Are we this instant immortal or mortal? Are we this instant indwelling in God — His image and likeness — or are we separated from Him and unlike Him in character?

Are we this instant incorporeal or corporeal? Are we this instant universal or finite and local? Are we this instant spiritually individual or personal? Is our state of thought the truth or is it malpractice, which is the denial of Truth? Mrs. Eddy says in *Miscellany*, "Unless you fully perceive that you are the child of God, hence perfect, you have no Principle to demonstrate and no rule for its demonstration."

The Christian Scientist who stands fast in the oneness of God and man, and knows there is no man unlike and apart from God, his divine Principle, and knows there is no man with any other mind than the one and only Mind — this Christian Scientist with his pure thought is looking through and beyond the mist of the mere appearance of man into the realm of the real. He beholds and knows that all false appearance is but the hidden existence of good, just as the mirage lake is the hidden existence of the prairie grass.

Uncover Error as Nothing

We have all been instructed in the letter and spirit of Christian Science, and we are equipped to carry on a treatment against malpractice. But we cannot give a good treatment if we believe there is a mind to work against us or injure us. We must designate mental malpractice purely as belief, and never permit it to assume any reality whatsoever in our consciousness. Our textbook tells us, "Until the fact concerning error — namely its nothingness — appears, the moral demand will not be met, and the ability to make nothing of error will be wanting."

We need to remind ourselves that error is always to be uncovered as nothingness, and is never uncovered until the nothingness of the error is apparent. This is as true of the error called malpractice, as it is of any other error. Error is never uncovered except as nothing. So long as there appears to be reality to that which we call error, just so long error is still covered. There are times when we find it necessary to argue against the claims of evil, but the arguments used are valueless unless they result in a clear realization of the nothingness of error.

True practice uncovers any and all error — that is, true practice destroys the belief in error. But we cannot remind ourselves too frequently that the process by which this occurs should progressively become more spiritualized. There should be less of the human element and more of the divine presence in the work of uncovering error. In reality it is the allness of Truth which makes nothing of error. Therefore, as workers in Christian Science, our conscious sense of Science must be that of Spirit — that is to say, our thought must not merely be *about* Truth, our thought must *be* Truth. *When our thought is Truth, then error is nothing.*

Disease is error. Then, when we are asked to take a case of sickness, we consider it error — nothing less and nothing more. Even when that which confronts us appears as wickedness in some form or other, even when it appears as malicious thought or harmful personality, we deal with it as error or nothingness — no thing, no person. There is no other way to deal with error effectually. Mrs. Eddy says, "Evil has no reality. It is neither person, place, nor thing, but is simply a belief, an illusion of material sense."

All affirmations and denials that we make, however elaborate, have for their sole object the realization of the omnipotence, omniscience and omnipresence of God, Principle, Love; and we are justified in the use of these words only by the result obtained from their use. We, as Christian Scientists, should present unquestionable proofs of the healing and protective results of our work.

Protective Work

A part of the daily work of every Christian Science student is protection against the possible belief in trouble of any name or nature. And where is this protective work to be done? Protective work is always done in the realm of belief. We should see that mortal mind, with all its beliefs of destructiveness and loss and accident, cannot become a part of our consciousness or anybody's consciousness. That we should constantly know and constantly prove the protective power of omnipotence, need hardly be stated.

Our protective work should definitely annul the belief in medical science, together with those of the undertaker, and all other phases of error which claim that every human being must ultimately fall into their hands.

We, as workers in Christian Science, should have the conscious sense of the substance and allness of Spirit, and consequent realization of the unreality of matter, and the unreality of a material personality. Without such a realization, we do not fulfill the metaphysical requirements. We should associate ourselves with the infinity of good, and never believe that in so doing we shall fail in any degree to manifest humanly all that is good for us and for others. Mind is one and infinite. Mind has no competitor. Nothing is comparable to Mind, for Mind is All. An apprehension of this fact is essential to the handling of any phase of malpractice.

3. HEALING BY MEANS OF
CHRISTIAN SCIENCE TREATMENT

In the French edition of *Der Herold der Christian Science* of May 1936, there is a reprint of an excerpt from a letter written in 1902 by Mrs. Eddy to one of her students. It reads as follows: "Healing is the best sermon, healing is the best lecture, and is the entire demonstration of Christian Science. The sinner and the sick healed are our best witnesses." From another letter written in 1904 to a student, she says, "Beloved student, as I understand it, God has His Cause demonstrated in healing the sick. Jesus taught this." And from a letter dated 1896, she says, "To know that there is but one God, one cause, one effect, one Mind, heals instantly. Have but one God and your reflection of Him does the healing."

In *Science and Health* she writes, "Whoever reaches the understanding of Christian Science in its proper signification will perform the sudden cures of which it is capable; but this can be done only by taking up the cross and following Christ in the daily life." In the *Manual of the Mother Church* she writes: "Healing the sick and the sinner with Truth demonstrates what we affirm of Christian Science, and nothing can substitute this demonstration. I recommend that each member of this Church shall strive to demonstrate by his or her practice, that Christian Science heals the sick quickly and wholly, thus proving this Science to be all that we claim for it."

In *Science and Health* Mrs. Eddy says: "Love for God and man is the true incentive in both healing and teaching." In this statement, we plainly see that love for man stands side by side with love for God, and is of the utmost importance in both healing and teaching. Healing is the keynote of Christian Science. We as students of Christian Science need to be constantly awake to the fact that the healing of sickness and sin established the church, and today nothing less than the healing of sickness and sin will maintain

34

the church, and accomplish the purpose for which the church was designed.

When we, as Christian Scientists, permit the organization which is called the church to become our chief concern, we are entering upon the downward path toward extinction, which today seems to threaten the Protestant churches of the world. The healing of sickness and sin, which is our demonstration of Christian Science, should be the first and practically the only consideration of any Christian Science student; and the church organization will progress in the exact proportion that the healing of sickness and sin is the mission of the church.

There is no greater work than the healing work, and to relegate the healing work to a secondary place, and devote our time and attention wholly to so-called worldly problems is erroneous. We, as students of Christian Science, should beware of the suggestion that we should set aside the healing work for ourselves and others for a greater work. There is no greater work than the perfect and permanent healing of disease and sin through divine power, which is made available to us through Christian Science.

More and more it becomes a truism that we can demonstrate through Christian Science only that which is already eternally true and real. This fact that we can demonstrate only what is eternally true, differentiates Christian Science from all other healing systems, and requires on the part of Christian Scientists a recognition and demonstration of divine actualities, with nothing weighing in the balance against these actualities. In this way only can the steadfastness of purpose, which Christian Science demands of its adherents, be maintained with the glow of divine enthusiasm.

What Is It That Heals?

What is it that heals sickness and sin? A pure, clear realization of Truth is what heals. Who gives the treatment? Divine Mind gives the treatment. The thoughts and ideas in any treatment are not formed by a personal mind, but they have their source and

35

being in divine Mind and are Truth. We should always keep our treatment God, Mind, Truth. We should let our treatment be Truth, and not merely a personal effort. In every case, we should handle the different phases from the standpoint of God — for God is All.

What is it that heals sickness and sin? Our very presence heals sickness and sin. I do not mean our personal presence, because our presence is never personal. Mind, God, Truth, gives us presence. We are omnipresence, and this omnipresence is omniscience, or all-knowing. Omniscience knows all, and knows there is no sickness or sin. No sickness or sin, and no belief of sickness or sin, can reside in omnipresence or omniscience. I AM THAT I AM is all there is to Mind, and therefore is all there is to His presence — man.

What is treatment? Mind knows and what He knows is treatment. What Mind knows is our knowing, and is our treatment. We should clearly understand that what we know is not our personal knowing, it is not a knowing apart and dissociated from Mind. Our treatment is just I AM THAT I AM. We should never permit our personal self to get between God and our case. In real treatment, there is no practitioner and no patient — there is just God present, expressed as the real man or as all divine ideas.

To all intents and purposes, treatment is God, Mind, in full operation as divine law, or the truth of being. The affirmations and realizations of the so-called practitioner should not merely be *about* Truth — they must *be* Truth; they must *be* the Christ of God, His omnipresence, the real man wholly mental and spiritual.

Our Attitude of Thought Toward Persons

When giving a treatment, what should be our attitude towards persons? We should get rid of persons; we should not think of persons either sick or well. There is no person involved in the case. What appears to be a person afflicted by disease, is the son of God, divine in being and divine in his attributes.

From our Christian Science textbook we learn that to believe there is a person afflicted with disease, and then to try to heal that person through a Christian Science treatment, is mental quackery. And to see man, woman, child, or anyone or anything as an actual patient needing healing, is also mental quackery. (See *Science and Health* 395:21). Personality is only a belief — the belief that man is a mortal, personal existence, instead of the ever-presence of divine Mind as divine intelligence.

In one of Mrs. Eddy's unpublished statements relative to what we should know about a patient, she said: "Know that a divine idea has come to be recognized, rather than a sick person to be healed. There is no sick man with a sick body, or a sick mind, or a sick head, or a sick organization anywhere seeking help or needing it." And, students, how could there be a sick person, since God and man are one being, and this one being is infinite, indivisible all?

In another of Mrs. Eddy's unpublished statements concerning the practitioner's state of thought, she said: "To look out into the world and see sin, sickness and death: that is hate. To look out into the world and see everything in God's image and likeness: that is Love." This statement was a great revelation to me. I clearly saw that when I, as a practitioner, look out into the world and see sin, sickness and death, it is because I, as yet, am carnal in my thought, and therefore in belief I am manifesting the quality of hate. But when I, as a practitioner, clearly understand that my mind is infinite Love, and that infinite Love is universal in its scope, then when this Love that I am, looks out into the world, it can see nothing but itself. In all the world, Love can see nothing but its own image and likeness. "Love inspires, illumines, designates, and leads the way," our textbook tells us.

Students, after we have treated a patient, then what do we do? In substance, I shall tell you what my teacher told me. He said: "Having treated your patient, and having removed from your own thought all envy, all hatred, all pride, then stand in the consciousness of Truth." I clearly saw that I could not stand in the consciousness of Truth and have anything in my heart unlike Truth. We, as students of Christian Science, should stand in our treatment in an attitude of Truth. It is Truth that heals.

Practical Hints for Treatment

There are three things in every treatment that we should always handle — *cause, substance, law*. There is no cause to disease; there is no substance for disease to manifest itself upon; there is no law that supports disease. Man and the universe are spiritual, because all cause is Spirit, or Mind. The flower, bird, tree, landscape, rock, house, stomach, eye, hand, arm, head, all are spiritual. Their cause, substance, and law is Spirit. Mortals, by placing cause, substance, and law as matter and material, of necessity view all things from a material point of view, and this is why things appear material, sick, decaying, and dying.

In our treatment, what should we handle to avoid a relapse or a return of the claim? We should handle astrology. That is, we should handle the mass-mesmerism or universal belief that man was born. Man was never born. The demonstration and proof of this fact is in Mind, and cannot get out of Mind. There is no selfhood apart from Mind. Our real selfhood is in oneness and unity with Mind, and is there eternally. A treatment of this nature frees consciousness from fear, self-love, self-pity, self-depreciation, self-condemnation, and the mesmerism of disease.

There can be no relapse. The healing that has taken place stands, because the wholeness that has appeared is the evidence of God's presence. There is no temporary or superficial healing. A case cannot be partially or superficially healed, because this individual manifestation of God is already whole and has always been whole.

What shall we do about the condition that we have treated a long time? In such instances the patient's thought has become mesmerized, and to heal such a case we must know that our treatment, which is Truth, must dominate the patient; and that our thought, which is Mind's thought, is the only mentality going on under our treatment. What we know as Truth about the case is the Christ, and is the healing power.

When a belief continues just as though no treatment were given, what is the trouble? When treatment is given, and the belief goes on just as if no treatment were given, there is some phase of error that is not recognized, and therefore not handled. That a Christian Science treatment can be ineffective, is a suggestion that we should not ignore. In such cases, the one under treatment may intellectually see that error is an impossibility, and yet be accepting the seeming error as something. Unconsciously there may be the feeling that error will be nothing when it is once destroyed, but as yet he believes it is undestroyed.

God gave man dominion, and our dominion consists in recognizing reality — in knowing that which is, and in perceiving the nothingness of nothing. It takes an altitude of understanding to perceive the nothingness of nothing, and usually the patient wants to call error something, and leave the practitioner to perceive the nothingness of something. If error ever were something, we could not perceive the nothingness of it. We cannot heal or deal with nothing, and until this particular image of error is extinguished in human consciousness, the belief will continue.

How long should we continue to treat a case? We should continue until the case is healed, providing there is evidence of some improvement. How long? 'Long' is a word that relates to time, and time has nothing to do with Christian Science healing. Every treatment that is given, should be given as if it were the only treatment ever to be given to the case.

In the work of a practitioner, there should never be the thought that it might be necessary to give another treatment. And no practitioner is living up to the actual requirements of Christian Science who, while treating a case, holds to the belief that no matter how much the patient is helped, the patient is destined to die sometime. A treatment, or any number of treatments, given from this standpoint, is wanting in the character and nature which gives divine power to the treatment.

All Christian Scientists Practice Christian Science

Christian Scientists practice Christian Science. This is true of Christian Scientists who are engaged in other professions and business occupations, as well as those practicing Christian Science exclusively. We who practice Christian Science are establishing facts, and a treatment — no matter what its nature — brings about a change of consciousness that makes us better Christian Scientists. To maintain thought that is merely *like* divine being is not sufficient; thought that is actuality and law and the presence of the divine being is demanded of every Christian Science worker. This is what Mrs. Eddy calls "practical, operative Christian Science."

We as students have entered the path, and our growth demands not mere argument, wherein Truth and error seem to be forever contending. It requires of us a willingness to work, an endeavor to achieve, and a consequent ability to deal with and to heal every form of evil, not from the standpoint of the seeming evil, but from the standpoint of the omnipotence and omnipresence of good.

Since the object of Christian Science is redemption of thought, quite as much as physical healing, there are many instances where treatment going on for a long time is essential, and in such cases there should be no question of time. There is no limit to the redemptive power of Christian Science. Mrs. Eddy says in the textbook: "Signs and wonders are wrought in the metaphysical healing of physical disease; but these signs are only . . . to attest the reality of the higher mission of the Christ-power to take away the sins of the world."

Those who take up the study of Christian Science desire to attain the facts of Christian Science. The study is on the part of the patient or student, but the explanation of Christian Science often comes through the practitioner or teacher who brings about an awakening which is a veritable new birth. This redemptive work, in many cases, may be quite prolonged; but the triumphs of Truth far out balance the hopes deferred.

Jesus, when here among us, did not tell us to talk the truth, or to think about the truth. He said, *Know the truth*. And, students, the truth that makes us free is the truth that we are already free.

THE AGE OF DIVINE INTELLIGENCE
Association Address of 1942

1. Service and Love: Essential Elements
of Christianity ... 45

2. Our Mission in the World Is Individual ... 48

3. The Age of Divine Intelligence ... 54

4. Our Practice Governed by Our Viewpoint ... 62

5. Idealism and Realism ... 65

6. Deflection ... 69

7. Supply ... 74

8. Business ... 78

9. Money ... 88

10. I AM ... 90

THE AGE OF DIVINE INTELLIGENCE
Association Address of 1942

by

Martha Wilcox

1. SERVICE AND LOVE
ESSENTIAL ELEMENTS OF CHRISTIANITY

Dear Students: I heartily welcome you, one and all, on this occasion. Our association day should be not only a joyous experience, but also a very sacred one. This day should be made holy by our association with our own divine Mind, as well as by our association with each other. And we should remember that those we call 'others' are our own divine Mind expressed. The thought of each individual student should be kept inviolate, free from any hurt on this day.

The first association of students — Jesus with his disciples — was held in a little upper room in Jerusalem. It was there that Jesus taught his disciples the essential elements of Christianity — *service and love*. And after the test of centuries, service and love are still the essential elements of Christianity.

At this first association meeting, Jesus washed the disciples' feet and said, "I am among you as he that serveth." He also said, "A new commandment I give unto you, That ye love one another." Then he explained to them that they were not to love according to the personal sense of love, but "as I have loved you, that ye also love one another." Jesus impressed upon the thought of his disciples that individually they were to love all others, as all

45

others are in Truth. To love others as Jesus loved them, is to be that conscious love that is so mighty in power that it heals the sick, forgives sin, and raises the dead.

The students at this first association meeting needed to be changed in their natures in order to serve and love as did the Master. At this meeting, the power of Truth was so irresistible that the natures of these students were changed; and they gladly obeyed the command, and went forth to teach and to heal and to establish the Christian church.

Centuries later, another association of students was held — a few students with their teacher, Mary Baker Eddy. Again, the same essential elements of Christianity — service and love — were given to this little group of students. And likewise, the nature of these students was changed; and the spirit of Truth which wrought these changed natures involved the divine power that enabled these students to go forth to teach, to heal, to forgive sin, to raise the dead, and to establish in the world divine Science, or the church of Christian Science.

On that first association day, Christianity, through its elements of service and love, was given to the world. On the second association day, the same Christianity, still expressed as service and love, was revealed to the world in a higher degree as divine Science. And today, this same Christianity, through service and love, is culminating in the demonstration of divine Science, which is the coming of the Son of man, both individually and universally.

We may ask, "What is our relation to this unfolding event — the coming of the Son of man?" There would be no such event today, were it not for the individual student of Christian Science. Individually we are the coming of the Son of man. The demonstration of divine Science, or the coming of the Son of man, is the appearing of higher, truer qualities of service and love within the individual mentality.

The time is at hand when we, as adherents of divine Science, must demonstrate and give proof to the world that "all nations are of one blood," that is, all nations and all peoples, when correctly understood, are of one Mind. God is their Maker. All nations and all peoples are the one divine Mind expressed; and we, individually, must be that conscious love that sees all nations and all peoples as they are in Truth.

When this seeming mental conflict called war has spent itself, and we have given to the world the proof of the supremacy of mental and spiritual power over so-called physical power, there will be present a great need for prepared workers — workers who can teach and heal, and help others to gain an understanding of divine Science.

How does this spiritual power come to the individual student? Spiritual power comes through our individual responsiveness to Truth. In the proportion that we are responsive to Truth, and let Truth be present in us, there is also present actual spiritual power. And all material resistance will disappear from our consciousness in the proportion that we free ourselves from the false claims of error.

Today should be our Pentecostal Day — the day on which we are filled with spiritual power, or filled with the Holy Ghost. If there is any feeling of disturbance in our thought today; if there is any bitterness, dislikes, or aversion to anyone or anything in all the world; if there is a clouded past or any anxiety for the future — let it all vanish into its native nothingness; and let us breathe in silent prayer the words of our beloved Leader, "Fill us today with all thou art — be thou our saint, our stay, alway."

What are the vital points in this prayer? Not only service and love for mankind, but the great need of being responsive to Truth only. In this way material resistance to Truth is nothing, and we are free to reflect spiritual power.

2. OUR MISSION IN THE WORLD IS INDIVIDUAL

In our work today, I shall speak much of the individual; I shall stress the importance of the individual; and I shall emphasize the need of the individual doing much metaphysical work within himself. Scientifically speaking, there is no one else but himself for whom the individual can work. Scientifically speaking, we as individual man include the universe, or we include all others and everything within our individual self, and as our individual self.

When we see what we call another, we see somewhat of ourselves. And in order to respect and love ourselves or individual man we must respect and love others. In order to serve others we must likewise serve ourselves. As we, individually, are lighted with Truth and Love, we find that our whole world of people and things within ourselves is automatically lighted. There is nothing external to our individual consciousness. All men in unity is the one Christ within us, is individual man — our real selves.

It has been said or written, "Thou must be true thyself, if thou the truth wouldst teach; thy heart must overflow, if thou another's heart wouldst reach," and Mrs. Eddy emphatically tells us that Truth must be written first on the tablet of one's own heart in order to serve one's self, and in this way to serve others.

During the past few years, the Christian Scientists have prayed and worked and struggled to disperse the truth of Christian Science throughout the world; but today we are praying and striving as never before to gain a rapid spiritual growth within ourselves. Why? Because today it is demanded of the Christian Scientist that he be so clear in his mentality that he is able to translate every phase of human life into reality, and to give concrete proof of healing and salvation to a sick and war-torn world.

Each Christian Science practitioner and student should be so filled with the spirit of service and love that he can instantly answer the urgent call for help. But such proofs can be given only by those individuals in Christian Science whose natures are transformed through prayer — righteous prayer, fervent prayer, prayer as understood in Christian Science, which is "an absolute faith that all things are possible to God."

Prayer

Mrs. Eddy speaks with emphasis about prayer. In *Miscellaneous Writings*, she says, "One thing I have greatly desired, and again earnestly request, namely that Christian Scientists, here and elsewhere, pray daily for themselves, not verbally, nor on bended knee, but mentally, meekly, and importunately." Do we as individuals pray daily for *ourselves*? Not for someone else, nor for something else, but for ourselves? Jesus is our example, and he spent hours in prayer.

First, Mrs. Eddy requests us to pray mentally. I wonder if we really understand how blessed we are to be able to pray mentally, how blessed we are that our individual mind, through the enlightenment of Truth, can become a state of spiritual understanding wherein Christ, or individual man, is the only man.

Second, Mrs. Eddy requests us to pray with a spirit of meekness; that is, we are to pray and realize and understand with the sense of peace and sureness that David had when, without armor or sword, he slew Goliath. David spoke with a sense of meekness when he said, "Thou comest to me with a sword, and with a spear, and with a shield: but I come to thee in the name [meaning the character] of the Lord of hosts . . . for the battle is the Lord's." When we pray meekly, our state of mind is one of calmness and sureness and innocence — a state of pure consciousness wherein the reciprocal law of being is in operation universally. Daniel, when in the lions' den, understood this reciprocal law of being. His mind was not dual. He did not believe that his mind was God's presence, and also believe there was a wicked king and ferocious beasts outside his mind.

Daniel, because of his conscious oneness and completeness and perfection with divine Mind, knew that he included the king and the lions of God's creating within himself. And Daniel knew that the king and the lions, because of their conscious oneness and completeness and perfection with divine Mind, included him within themselves. The king and the lions were in Daniel's completeness and perfection, and Daniel made up something of the king's and lions' completeness and perfection.

Daniel knew that God, or Mind, was verified in that very place as One and All. He knew that he and the king and the lions were reciprocal to each other, and that each and all were governed by God's reciprocal law of being. It was Daniel's sureness of this reciprocal law of infinite good that dispelled the seeming evil in his individual consciousness and the consciousness of the king and the lions.

Third, Mrs. Eddy requests us to pray importunately, that is, insistently. When our need is great, when we are sorely perplexed, when our whole heart and being yearn to be uplifted — then we are to pray importunately. Jesus prayed importunately and then Lazarus came forth from the grave. To pray importunately does not mean to reach out and up desperately to some power outside of ourselves. To pray importunately is our own persistent and insistent effort to be that state of truth, or understanding, or realization that is the Christ — the real man that we already are.

In the proportion that we pray daily for ourselves — that is, pray mentally, meekly, importunately, as the occasion demands — we gain spiritual growth rapidly. It might be well for each individual here today to look deep into his own heart, and see if he really desires rapid spiritual growth, and if he is earnestly striving and praying for it. If we really desire rapid spiritual growth, we must work and pray to accomplish two things. First, *we must dematerialize matter*; second, *we must impersonalize personality*.

Do we understand that what we call matter is merely a phase of mortal mind? Do we understand the illusory character of matter? Do we understand that matter never is substance, never is presence, and never occupies space? Do we understand that matter is nonexistent, nothing? Do we understand that matter cannot do anything to us, and that we cannot do anything to matter, any more than the horizon can do something to us, or we can do something to the horizon? Matter is like the horizon; it is delusion, deception, false appearance only, a false image in the human mind. To dematerialize matter, we must see to it that our individual consciousness is not active as these phases of mortal thought. In the practice of Christian Science, there is nothing more important than the dematerialization of matter.

The qualities of mortal mind which seem to make matter something are the qualities that we call density, finiteness, boundary, divisibility, mutability, destructibility, separability, mortality — qualities which are unknown and unthinkable to conscious Mind. By dematerialization (by taking all these qualities or characteristics from persons and things), we have left only divine ideas or real man. We find it no small task to dematerialize matter, and it seems an even greater task to impersonalize our beliefs in personality; but in order to grow spiritually, we must understand that personality is belief only, a false phase of mortal thought. Personality, like matter, has no real existence. Personality is a lie, or false concept, about our true individuality.

How do we impersonalize our belief in finite personality? We do it by stripping a so-called personality of all the qualities and characteristics that seem to constitute a personality — the qualities and characteristics of finiteness, corporeality, physicality, mortality, organic existence, etc. When we impersonalize these qualities and strip them from a so-called personality, we find at hand the individual man, the real man, still seen as our true humanhood.

Jesus impersonalized his belief of personalities when he encountered the multitude. How did Jesus do this? It is recorded that he went at once up into the mountain — or a high altitude of understanding — that he might unsee the demands of these seeming many minds or many personalities.

51

When we encounter the multitude, do we not see the multitude with its beliefs as external to us? Do we not at times go to greet the multitude, and try to meet its demands through human efforts and human responsibilities? Do we not sometimes even try to manage persons? Jesus did not do so. He went at once to a higher understanding of individual man, and we should do likewise. The multitude is always a false concept within our own mentality, and it is through our own wisdom, Truth, and Love, that we see individual man as the only man present. It is the Christ within us that dispels the belief in personality, and sees the Christ, or real man, in others.

Benevolence

In speaking of benevolence, it is far from my thought to belittle the support of our church organization. The maintenance of the Christian Science church organization is a duty and privilege of each individual Christian Scientist. But there is a marked tendency on the part of the Christian Scientist to substitute personal benevolence for scientific demonstration. Scientific demonstration in the matter of benevolence is a within process, wherein we see Christ, or individual man, present in his fullness and completeness. Scientific demonstration permits of no belief of depletion for anyone or anything, but reveals a greater fullness for the whole world.

Peter and John set an example for all of us in spiritual giving. They said to the lame man at the gate of the temple, "Silver and gold have I none; but such as I have give I thee: in the name of Jesus Christ of Nazareth rise up and walk." Peter and John gave what each man owes his brother — the recognition of him as God's own image. Such Christly perception heals and saves and is the greatest benevolence there is.

There is a marked tendency to bestow our goods upon others without a proper provision for ourselves, which often results in self-depletion. To be neglectful of one's own self under the guise of unselfishness, is not the way of wisdom. This is letting our benevolence drop to the level of a personal giver and a personal receiver. It is a far greater sense of benevolence to understand that man moves in reciprocal relation to every other idea. Man receives all that God gives and through reflection gives all that he receives. We are being most benevolent when we refuse to accept the personal sense testimony of limitation and poverty, and understand that man consciously exists at the standpoint of infinity.

There are many students in the association who are entering the practice of Christian Science. It is always well to do earnest praying in regard to taking patients. Not everyone who is sick is ready for Christian Science, or even desires the spiritual awakening which is necessary for complete healing. Jesus counseled selectivity. He said to his disciples, "Go not into the way of the Gentiles (meaning those who did not want to worship God), and into any city of the Samaritans (meaning any evil consciousness), enter ye not. But go rather to the lost sheep of the house of Israel (meaning those who are trying to find the way)." We wrong our Cause when the choosing of our patients is not of divine guidance. Mrs. Eddy says in *Science and Health*, "Millions of unprejudiced minds — simple seekers for Truth, weary wanderers, athirst in the desert — are waiting and watching for rest and drink. Give them a cup of cold water in Christ's name and never fear the consequences."

The vital points of this subject of our individual mission are:

1. Our mission in the world is as individual as Jesus' mission or Mrs. Eddy's mission. And we should be supremely content in the self-knowledge that we are fulfilling our individual mission in the world.
2. Our natures can be transformed only through prayer.
3. We should understand and use the reciprocal law of being.
4. We should dematerialize matter and impersonalize personality.

3. THE AGE OF DIVINE INTELLIGENCE

We are studying a Science that requires intelligence, and requires the cultivation of intelligence. Intelligence is divine, and without limit; it is the most natural thing to our being. There is nothing in the whole world that is of so much worth to the individual as his intelligence. Do we recognize its worth? Do we recognize its source? Do we even think enough about it to be grateful for it?

There is no other definition in the chapter "Recapitulation" that means so much to the student as the definition of intelligence. Mrs. Eddy asks, "What is intelligence?" Then she answers, "Intelligence is omniscience, omnipresence, omnipotence. It is the primal and eternal quality of infinite Mind, of the triune Principle — Life, Truth, and Love, — named God." (*Science and Health*) Have we studied this definition? Have we thought it out? Many of us do much reading, but very little thinking.

As we understand our intelligence for what it really is, we shall be able to think things out, and to do things that we have never been able to do before. We have entered a new age, and this new age will be recorded in history as an era of divine intelligence — an incoming of mental strength and mental loveliness. Since mankind is being awakened to the divine source, origin, and character of his so-called human intelligence, this new age will be characterized by unusual mental and spiritual phenomena.

What is the nature of intelligence? Intelligence, to itself, is consciously one thing, namely God — the unity of Life, Truth, and Love. Intelligence sees itself as one whole, as both subject and object. It sees and knows itself as being all intelligence, sees and knows its own universe of divine intelligence.

The definition of intelligence gives us a correct understanding of the character of God, or Mind. The character of God, or Mind, is divine intelligence, just as the character of the sun is light. We do not think of Mind as producing intelligence; Mind *is* intelligence.

We are not separate from God — our own Mind — and since God, our Mind, is divine intelligence, we are not separate from this divine intelligence. We show forth divine Mind — our own divine intelligence. Wherever individual man is, there divine intelligence is in its divine being and divine manifestation.

When we think of God, or Mind, correctly, we think of an infinite, loving, active, conscious mode of divine intelligence. And when we think of man correctly, we think of this infinite mode of divine intelligence in manifestation as man. Man consciously identifies this infinite mode of divine intelligence. God and man are one in their character and being, and we think of this unity, or oneness, as divine intelligence expressed as human intelligence. The manifestation cannot be separate from, or unlike the manifested. We do not think of man as a personal, material mortal man, but we think of man as a mode of intelligence in oneness with divine intelligence.

The mind that we have is divine intelligence. Each one of us is this one divine intelligence in manifestation. If we comprehend the fact that our own Mind, our God, is divine intelligence, all sin, disease, lack, age and death would be unknown. Since divine intelligence, the all-knowing, cannot consciously be the knowledge or experience of sin, disease, lack, age, or death, then such experiences cannot be in manifestation as intelligence, or man.

The substance and being of everything in the universe is divine intelligence. The heart, liver, lungs and blood, in their substance and being, are living, conscious modes of divine intelligence. Since this is true, we could not think of heart, liver, lungs, and blood as matter, as finite, changeable, and destructible; but we should understand them as they are in reality — as divine intelligence, and then think what divine intelligence is in fact.

We have been taught to believe that each individual has a mind of his own, called human intelligence. We have been taught to believe that this human intelligence is disconnected from God and can be both good and evil. But in this new age of divine intelligence, a phenomenon of the first magnitude has appeared, and gives proof that the intelligence of man is not human or personal, but is primarily divine intelligence.

When correctly understood, our so-called human intelligence is a holy thing, entirely good. Our so-called human intelligence is the presence of divine intelligence, or divine intelligence in manifestation. We, as Christian Scientists, are proving that all things that are good, useful and natural to the human intelligence have their source, origin, substance and being in divine intelligence. Indeed, all good, useful, natural things are divine intelligence appearing as these things in some degree of their reality.

What seems to be evil in the so-called human intelligence is not intelligence. The seeming evil has no principle; it has no motive power to carry it on; it is a misconception, a perversion, a deflection of some good and eternal fact in divine intelligence. Evil is nothing. It comes to us for its existence, and we give it all the existence it has. Through an understanding of divine Science, we prove that evil is nonexistent, and that the one infinite divine intelligence is eternal, unchangeable — the All and Only.

The true evaluation of our so-called human intelligence as being divine intelligence, is appearing in divine order as the wonder of this new age. This divine intelligence is appearing humanly and rapidly as an infinite variety and diversity of things — things of every sort and kind and description. As yet, we see this divine intelligence in its infinite manifestation imperfectly, or we see it with material accompaniments. But in the proportion that we discern the divine character of our human intelligence, the unfoldment of divine infinite intelligence will be immeasurable to us.

There is so much noise and confusion at this present time, that the unillumined mind fails to see what is taking place in the mental and spiritual realm. To those of clearer vision, this mental and spiritual phenomenon is appearing as higher and more efficient modes of intelligence, which are being brought out in visible, practical forms along all walks of life.

There is an insistent demand that we, as human beings, express a higher and more active intelligence. We are intelligent human beings only as we express divine intelligence. And in the measure that we express divine intelligence, we are not human beings, but are divine beings.

The divine intelligence which God, or Mind, expresses is man. This divine intelligence is the Son of God, and appears to human comprehension as the coming of the Son of man. This divine intelligence, or the coming of the Son of man, appears as higher, truer modes of thought or intelligence within ourselves. And in this new age, our demonstration of divine Science — visible as divine intelligence — is appearing not only to the individual, but universally as well.

Are we, as Christian Scientists, responsive to this insistent demand from within? Do we express, visibly and concretely, the higher modes and fuller unfoldments of divine intelligence? Or do we remain in the old grooves of thought until we bury ourselves? Of one thing we may be certain, we either respond to this urgent call from within, and become more active and alert in our thought, or we stagnate and die.

Uncovering of False Beliefs

As the facts of divine intelligence are better understood, and the human mind becomes illumined with the fact of its own divine intelligence, there takes place a great uncovering of false beliefs in the so-called human mind, and a corresponding desire to "free itself from self-imposed materiality and bondage."

A false belief of the human mind to be uncovered, is that all seeming troubles are *outside* of us, whereas in fact they are wholly *within* the human mind. These seeming troubles are purely mental, never physical. They are never apart nor outside of the human mind. Another false belief that is being uncovered is that the multitudinous troubles of the human mind are *personal troubles*, whereas in fact they are *impersonal errors* — simply deflections of reality. These troubles are states of thought that are, as yet, unillumined by divine intelligence.

Today, there is being uncovered and brought to our attention the many mental and emotional qualities, the traits of character, the attitudes of thought, and the natural tendencies of the individual. These are all being greatly stressed at this present time. Under the present world conditions, we have ample opportunity to note the false mental and emotional adjustment, the lack of mental and spiritual poise, and the great need of peace and harmony everywhere. These erroneous experiences are being uncovered to the so-called human mind, in order that we may correct them in our individual thinking. Take, for example, the mental agitations and disturbances we often experience when confronted with some unpleasant circumstance; or when others differ from our way of thinking and doing; or when we must do what we do not like to do; or when we read or hear of some dread disease; or when we fail to accomplish our desires. All these false emotions are not personal, but are the deflections of the one and only emotion of divine intelligence. And when we correct our thought in regard to them, we must know that they are deflections only, and never facts of divine intelligence.

Mrs. Eddy once said to a group of us, that we should never permit ourselves to be emotional. She meant that we should never permit ourselves to react with intensity to every seemingly unpleasant thing. She meant that we should so discipline our individual thought with the truth of being until we could stand in the presence of seeming error, mentally unmoved and steadfast in our faith in divine intelligence. And why should we be moved by that which is deflection only?

Mrs. Eddy says in the "Foreword" to *The First Church of Christ, Scientist*, and *Miscellany*, "The helpfulness of consistent right thinking — intelligent thinking untainted by the emotionalism which is largely self-glorification — is a reasonable service which all Christian Scientists can render their Leader."

When we, as students of Christian Science, fail to overcome these false mental modes of chronic emotions through the higher, truer modes of divine intelligence, they result in harmful effects on our health; they incapacitate us for efficient work; and they prevent us from being citizens of strength and usefulness. Nearly every page of our textbook shows us the necessity of watching our mental states and emotions. In it we read, "Lurking error, lust, envy, revenge, malice, or hate will perpetuate or even create the belief in disease." To these we might add irritability, criticism, egotism, anxiety, indecision, doubt, pride, self-pity, self-will, self-justification, fear, etc. If we have any of these mental modes or emotions, it is because our thoughts, feelings and actions are based upon the deflections as something, instead of being based upon divine intelligence as all.

Our textbook tells us, "We should examine ourselves and learn what is the affection and purpose of the heart, for in this way only can we learn what we honestly are." In *Miscellaneous Writings*, we read, "Learn what in thine own mentality is unlike 'the anointed,' and cast it out." And again, "Thought must be made better, and human life more fruitful, for the divine energy to move it onward and upward."

This uncovering of false modes of human intelligence is appearing not only to Christian Scientists, but is appearing universally to all planes of comprehension of the human mind. In this universal uncovering, "The earth helped the woman." By this we mean that there are many worthy psychologists, surgeons, physicians, and eminent ministers who are educating the unillumined thought to see that all causation is mental, and that all physical effects are the result of mental causes. The mental little foxes that spoil the vines are being uncovered to the human intelligence, and in a great degree the human thought is being prepared to accept the fact of one divine intelligence universally. In speaking of psychology let us bear in mind that there is only one Science of psychology. In *Miscellaneous Writings* Mrs. Eddy states: "Hence the deep demand for the Science of psychology to meet sin, and uncover it; thus to annihilate hallucination." And in our textbook, Mrs. Eddy speaks of the Science of psychology as "the Science of Spirit, God."

This Science of Spirit, or law of divine intelligence, is appearing to so-called human intelligence, and is there doing its effective work. The only psychology, the Science of Spirit, dispels hallucination in no other place than in the so-called human intelligence. What does the Science of psychology or the Science of divine intelligence uncover about alibis or excuses? These laws are uncovering to us that alibis and excuses are the natural tendencies in which the human mind indulges. Practically all of us use alibis and excuses, and sometimes quite unconsciously. We make them a smoke screen for our mistakes and failures and imperfections. Our pet alibis are, It was the other fellow's fault; It was an unavoidable circumstance; or We did not have a fair chance.

The harmful effect of alibis or excuses on the individual is far more serious than we realize. Many persons are in hospitals, even insane asylums, because they have hidden behind an alibi or an excuse until their so-called human intellect is enfeebled and impaired. They have permitted their headaches, their indigestion, their nerves, their belief in persons and circumstances, to be an alibi or excuse for something that was hard to do, or that they did not want to do, until they literally lost their power to decide things intelligently. An alibi or excuse is a form of deceit that is used to hide the facts in the case, and the results are most disastrous to the one who indulges in them.

In a book review of the magazine section of *The Christian Science Monitor*, there was a statement made by a noted surgeon. He said in substance that no organic cure could be permanent until a solution for the mental difficulties was found. He said that a lack of harmony in the realm of the spirit often leads to functional disorders and organic diseases, and that these could not be cured permanently until there was an adjustment of the underlying mental conflict.

Where is it that we, as individuals, contact and destroy error of every name and nature? Where do we contact the persons in the home, in business, in the church who seem to be thinking and acting erroneously? Where do we contact the unpleasant things to which we react so easily? It is not outside or apart from ourselves that we contact them. *We contact them within ourselves only, and at the point of our own belief in them.* At no other point than our own belief in them do we have contact with the claim of evil persons and unpleasant things. All temptations to believe in personality and in unpleasant things is at the point of our own belief in them, and here alone is where we overcome them. It is the duty of every Christian Scientist to examine his own mind, and take into strict account what is going on within his own mentality. Today, each one of us is being impelled to revamp his mental and emotional existence; each one of us is being forced to change his opinions and attitudes in order to tune in properly with the incoming of this new order of life — this age of divine intelligence.

Each student of Christian Science is required to hear with a new distinctiveness and understanding, and it is necessary to govern his thoughts and act accordingly. This new order of life is a divine order and is characterized as the age in which Christian Scientists are to give to the world the human proof of their divine and spiritual existence — the proof that we are now the sons and daughters of God, the expression of divine intelligence exempt from lack, age, decay, sin and death.

4. OUR PRACTICE GOVERNED BY OUR VIEWPOINT

Each Christian Science student should have a clearly defined mental position within himself. The patriarchs, prophets, Jesus, the disciples, and the Revelator, all held within themselves clearly defined mental positions from which they never swerved. Do we, as Christian Scientists, maintain a mental position in regard to our divine reality and our divine intelligence, from which we never swerve? The patriarchs and prophets based their mental positions on spiritual vision. What, to others of that time, seemed to be ordinary human conditions and events, these men interpreted according to spiritual vision, and placed upon these conditions and events an entirely different value than was placed on them by the mind that was unenlightened spiritually. These men lived life and practiced life based upon their spiritual vision of men and things, with the result that they exercised spiritual power. They brought water from the rock, they fed the hungry with barley loaves and corn, and raised the dead. They gave proof or evidence of their spiritual power.

This spiritual vision appeared in an enlarged measure to Jesus and the disciples in the form of the Holy Ghost, and they exercised enlarged spiritual power. And today this spiritual vision is appearing within our individual minds in a still larger unfoldment as divine Science. And we should exercise this power that is appearing to us as divine Science, or divine intelligence, and do the still "greater works."

Each one of us is living his life today either according to an incorrect viewpoint based upon material sense, or according to a viewpoint based upon divine Science. All the seeming troubles and inharmonies in the world today result from incorrect viewpoints, and we have these wrong viewpoints, because we base our interpretation of everybody and everything upon the beliefs of material sense. Wrong interpretation always results in a wrong viewpoint.

We have a correctly defined mental position, as did the patriarchs and Jesus, only as we base our mental position on a spiritual viewpoint and interpret man and the universe according to divine Science. It is through strict adherence to the laws of divine Science that we are able to interpret correctly every environment, circumstance, and event of our daily experience.

Jesus had a correct view of man. He not only interpreted man as man really is, but he gave instant proof or evidence of the perfect man at hand. Jesus had this correct view of man and things, and gave instant proof or evidence of wholeness and perfection, because he based his interpretations of man and things upon spiritual facts.

Do we interpret man as personal, and material, and mortal? Do we interpret the world in which we live as material and destructible? If we do, we are interpreting them erroneously, and are living our lives from the limited viewpoint of material sense. There is nothing wrong with our world, or with the people living in our world. It is our mental interpretation that is erroneous, and causes us to think and act from incorrect viewpoints. Every Christian Science student clearly understands that God is All and that His creation, man and the universe, is spiritual, eternal and perfect. This correct interpretation by the Christian Science student, gives instant proof as evidence, as in the days of Jesus, that the man and universe at hand are harmonious and eternal.

It is most important that we, as Christian Scientists, maintain a correct interpretation of ourselves and others and the things of our universe. Whatever we take cognizance of, and accept as fact, that becomes a part of what is ordinarily called our human consciousness, and is reflected in our body and in our affairs. If our viewpoint is determined by an incorrect interpretation of the divine fact at hand, then our bodies and our affairs reflect this false interpretation. But if our viewpoint is determined by a correct interpretation of true being, then our body and our affairs reflect the facts of divine Science.

With correct interpretation our human objectives are the objectification of true being. It takes a clearly defined mental position, based upon a correct viewpoint, to see orderliness in business, in world affairs, and in all activities. No change is needed in the external condition; but a change must take place in our mental position before we can maintain the sense of peace and joy that is strength and power, and that enables us to fulfill the needs of mankind.

When our individual interpretations are based on the facts of being, our thought is divine intelligence, and like the patriarchs of old, we see what the unillumined mind cannot see — a perfect world and harmonious experience. In the textbook Mrs. Eddy says, "Science reverses the evidence before the material senses and furnishes the eternal interpretation of God and man." As we exercise our thought and action from a viewpoint based upon the interpretation as given in divine Science, this new age will be for us an age of power, action, dominion and good works. It will be an age in which we, as individuals, give instantaneous proof or evidence of a perfect man and universe at hand. The vital points of this subject of our viewpoint as a student of Christian Science are:

1. We need within ourselves a clearly defined mental position from which we never swerve.
2. We should always, not sometimes but always, interpret man and the universe from the standpoint of divine Science, not from the standpoint of material sense.
3. Our viewpoint is reflected in our bodies, in our business, and in all of our affairs.

5. IDEALISM AND REALISM

Before taking up the subject of "Idealism and Realism," I wish to speak of a vital point that will help us to meet our so-called human needs — whether the need is health, a home, a position or tax money. It is most vital that we clearly understand that all divine ideas in our human mind are not just mere ideas, but eternal facts, and we should know and understand these ideas as infinite, eternal facts at hand.

There is only one Mind, and God, or Mind, expresses His own infinite being as ideas. These ideas are real and tangible. They are the only thing at hand. Everything that exists, everything that is good, useful and natural to human existence exists as a divine idea — a divine fact or entity, complete, finished, and is always at hand.

Error would always keep having two — a divine and a human concept about the divine idea. But we are learning that the human concept, or so-called material thing, is merely our imperfect apprehension of the divine idea, or only fact at hand. Mind evolves its own perfect ideas and their corresponding identities, and if my human sense calls these ideas a tree, a heart, a stomach, a house, tax money or a person, it makes no difference how they appear, the idea remains forever a divine fact at hand — perfect, immortal, and infinite as divine Mind. They are the phenomena of my spiritual consciousness and are my own self. If we wish to experience divine ideas in forms that will meet our daily needs, we must understand that each one of us is consciously this infinite compound of divine ideas. In the ratio that we understand that divine ideas have their source in divine Mind and are man, all human limitations will disappear.

We hear much these days about idealism and realism. It is easy for a Christian Scientist to be an idealist. And if our ideals have sufficient realization to control our conduct, then we are not only idealists, but we are also realists. When our idealism controls our conduct, it becomes realism. We are merely idealists when we are devoted to good and right ideas that to us are as yet unrealized thought, mere theories, intangible things — ideas that have not as yet been wrought out in life practice. We are merely idealists, because we do not clearly understand that all divine ideas are tangible things — eternal facts at hand.

As Christian Scientists, we should all be realists — that is, we should be devoted to ideas, and at the same time understand that all ideas within our minds are already realities, or eternal facts; and we should establish these ideas as facts in our thinking. And while these facts may not be fully embodied in our mind, we should see to it that they are in the process of being embodied in our mind, and embodied as fact. It is only when these ideas become realized thought, or visible tangible facts, that we can be called realists. As Christian Scientists, we have a vast accumulation of metaphysical ideas, good ideas, wonderful ideas. We affirm these ideas, and sometimes even exploit them; but much of the time they remain mere abstract ideas in thought. Many of us build up a world of metaphysical ideas, and still live in a world of unrealized thought. Why is this so? It is because we desire to escape the so-called problems of life, rather than work out the facts of life, and we take refuge in these metaphysical ideas in order to avoid our so-called problems.

There are no problems for us to escape from. The seeming problem is our imperfect apprehension of an actuality at hand. We have permitted our thought to dwell on this imperfect apprehension, and have accepted it as a reality, called it a problem, and then resisted it. We should realize that all so-called problems are some reality of being seen in reversion; and when we work out the so-called problem, we find a reality and reap a rich blessing.

Many of us iterate and reiterate statements of Truth, profound ideas, and think this reiteration will do for us what we must do for ourselves — that is, live these ideas out into facts or concrete experience. The repetition of ideas, as mere abstract ideas, acts upon the human mind as a mental narcotic, and weakens our power to demonstrate. This mere repetition of ideas has the tendency to make a weak student, instead of a strong one. We can repeat from *Science and Health* the scientific statement of being — the greatest statement of metaphysical fact — until it becomes a mere verbal statement, instead of a vital fact of power.

Since we are the infinite compound idea of Mind, it is quite right for us to possess an immeasurable number of metaphysical ideas. It is Godlike to have these ideas. But since the compound idea man is constituted of living, conscious ideas as facts, then it is logical that we should maintain all ideas as living, conscious facts, and not as mere abstract ideas.

Jesus was a realist. He possessed a wealth of ideas, but his ideas were to him living, conscious, concrete facts. When Jesus said, "The kingdom of heaven is within you," he did not mean that the kingdom was just a beautiful theory. Jesus meant that the kingdom of heaven is in us *now* as *a living, conscious fact*, and that we are to acknowledge this unseen fact, and identify with it concretely. Jesus showed forth the kingdom. He was the embodiment or the fulfillment of the fact of the kingdom of heaven. Jesus did not just express theories about life; he showed forth life, out of Life itself. Jesus answered the needs of the people, not only with the verbal statement of Truth, but with the demonstration or proof of present concrete facts at hand. Jesus' words and deeds were a unit. They were "the Word made flesh." When the idea of life was present in the consciousness of Jesus, the concrete evidence, or the fact of Life, was coincidentally present, so that he could say, "She is not dead, but sleepeth." And when the idea of money appeared as his consciousness, the concrete fact, which is eternally the idea, instantly appeared as the tax money.

Idealism in any subject never answers the needs of the people, and it will be a great help in growth when the inoperative idealism in Christianity is cleared away. Mrs. Eddy wrote, "Truth talked and not lived, rolls on the human heart a stone." Are we giving proof as evidence to the world that our bodies or environments, all circumstances and events connected with our lives, are divine facts at hand? It is our duty to present the concrete proof or evidence to the world, in order that the world may understand the spiritual facts of life. We must give the so-called material evidence to the world, since it is only the material evidence that mortal mind can understand. The Word, or idea, must be in evidence in the highest visible form that the human can comprehend.

To the world, the proof or evidence appears as improved material conditions; but to us who make the demonstration, the evidence is mental and spiritual. To us, the evidence may appear as a better body or a better business; but we understand that the evidence is our spiritual discernment that ideas are divine facts. Our idealism has become realism, and the proof or evidence is the result of our mental and spiritual understanding through which the Word becomes flesh. The vital points of this subject are:

> 1. Only that is really ours that we gain from the unfoldment of Truth or true ideas within ourselves. There is too much of reaching out for external ideas, instead of letting true ideas unfold from within. Let the marvelous truths or ideas in your textbook and your Quarterly Lessons unfold to you, and demonstrate them.
>
> 2. Reflect genuine joy and gladness and satisfaction in your daily living — "Joy in the Lord." The unfolding of true ideas within is your strength, and aids you in doing for mankind whatever is necessary to be done.

6. DEFLECTION

Our textbook contains many words that are not only vital in meaning, but a knowledge of which is essential to the student of Christian Science in working out the Science of being. One of these words is *deflection*.

Deflection, according to Webster, means to turn aside or to deviate from a true course. In Christian Science, deflection has reference to mortal man and to all that constitutes mortal man. Our textbook teaches that the untrue image of God, held in the human mind, is all there is to what we call mortal man. Then the correct sense of mortal man, is not an entity or an existence, but is an untrue image or deflection of the actual man at hand. Deflection results when the true appearance of actual man is turned aside or deviated by thought passing through a mind unillumined by Truth. This deviation of thought causes the actual man at hand to appear as sinning mortal man. The actual man is not changed, but his actuality is seen in reversion, or as deflection.

Deflection is an untrue image of actuality; and when in our practice work, we reverse this deflection or untrue image, in order to perceive actuality, we are using the process of thought that is set forth in our Christian Science textbook. When we understand deflection, we do not attach erroneous conditions to actual man, but we deal with the erroneous conditions as untrue images or deflections entirely separate and apart from actual man.

In the correct process of metaphysical work, we never have two things present. We understand that the actual thing is always present, and the deflected appearance does not make another thing. Spirit and matter are not two things. Spirit is the actual existence, and matter is the deflection or untrue image of Spirit. It is false appearance only. Actual man and sinning mortal man do not both exist. Actual man is, while sinning mortal man is the deflection or false appearance of actual man.

Actuality — the only thing that is at hand — does not need healing. It is God's very presence. The deflection, like the mirage lake, is nonexistent, and we cannot do anything to that which does not exist. A deflection, like the horizon, is not an entity nor a condition. It does not fill space. It is purely false appearance in the unillumined mind. When the prairie grass is seen as a mirage lake, we already understand that it is still prairie grass, and is not a lake. The prairie grass does not need anything done to it, regardless of how it appears. All there is to the mirage lake, is the prairie grass imperfectly seen. The mirage lake is nothing. It does not fill space and is nonexistent.

Deflections do not occupy space, and are never things or conditions. When we really understand this to be a fact, our work in Christian Science will be much easier. The deflection called a horizon does not fill space. All there is to the horizon is the earth and sky as they are in fact. Horizon is simply a name for that which does not fill space and is nonexistent. Likewise, the deflection called disease is just a name for that which does not occupy space, is not a thing or condition, and is nonexistent. Lack, and age, and fear are not conditions, and do not occupy space. They are deflections or untrue images of actuality.

The actuality of man, imperfectly seen, we have named personal man. The actuality of the universe, imperfectly seen, we have named the material universe. Now, we do not need to do anything to personal man or the material universe, but we do need to do something to our mode of mind that sees things as they are not. We need to enlighten our mind with the truth or fact of being. The mode of mind that sees deflection needs enlightenment.

Disarm the claim of personality. We should disarm — that is, render powerless — the deflection or false appearance of actual man that is called personality. Personality has neither life nor intelligence; it is mere ghost or shadow, and we should behold actual life and intelligence as Mind's omnipresence, where the ghost or shadow seems to be. Even though with our outer eyes we see personal man, the untrue image, with our inner spiritual vision we are to behold the actual man, the perfect man that Jesus beheld. With our spiritual thought we are to look through the deflections or illusions of matter, and behold the perfect ideas of divine intelligence.

Mrs. Eddy once went to call on a patient. After she had looked at the sick man, she turned away and went and looked out of the window, saying, "Dear heavenly Father, forgive me for looking at matter." The patient was instantly healed. If we see matter as anything other than a deflection of actual man, hence nonexistent, we are not practicing the laws of divine Science.

Mental Grooves

Unless we make earnest efforts through Christian Science to spiritualize our thought and to improve our thought processes, and strive to see actual man and the spiritual universe at hand, we are quite apt to lose the process of spiritual thinking altogether. Bicknell Young once said, "We often get into a rut and go right on in it." This might be said of many students and of some practitioners. They get into certain mental ruts or grooves, and go round and round in this fixed routine of thought, with the grooves growing deeper and deeper, until they bury themselves mentally. They have chained themselves to a fixed habit of thought. They have failed to spiritualize their thought and improve their mental processes; they have failed to see actual man and the spiritual universe at hand.

Demonstration depends upon improved processes. The demonstration of Christian Science depends upon the degree that we attain the Christ-mind, and upon our improved processes of thought. It takes the Christ-mind in us to see actualities at hand, where the deflections or false conditions seem to be. The Christ within does the healing. It is the spirit of Truth and Love — the Christ that is already the presence and substance of all things — that heals or dispels the deflections of mortal thought. We are not to save, or reform, or change that which appears to be personal man. Our mission is to give proof to the world that individual man — the actual man — is at hand. We are to give proof that man is not only in God's presence, but *is* God's presence.

As Christian Scientists, we should not desire to heal in the ordinary sense of healing. To desire to heal a claim or deflection is to have something in our thought besides actuality. But just to say there is nothing to heal, will not give proof that error or disease is not present. We must *be* the actual understanding in which there is no capacity to see or feel anything unlike the Christ-image. It is only as we have the Christ-mind, or sensible living Truth within ourselves as our own mind, that we can see the Christ, or the actuality of anyone or anything. When Peter said to Jesus, "Thou art the Christ," Jesus immediately answered Peter, "Flesh and blood [the personal mind] hath not revealed it unto thee." It was the Christ in Peter that could see Jesus as the Christ. (See Matt 16.)

The Claim of Age

I have been asked to say something about handling the claim of age. What is age? Where is age? Of one thing we may be sure, God is never aged, and His manifestation, actual man, is never aged. Then age is a deflection, an untrue image in the human mind. Age is not a condition to be healed, or to be dealt with; it is not a sense, and it is not a quality that belongs to God or to man. This deflection, or untrue image of thought called age, claims to out-picture itself as a sense of decline both in power and ability of all functions and faculties of the human life. It says there is deterioration or decadence of the substance of the so-called human body. Do we believe that God, Mind, Life, can consciously see or feel within itself what the human mind calls age? If God does not see or feel age, then actual man or body — the embodiment of all immortal ideas — cannot see, feel, show forth or experience the untrue image of age.

Mind, or conscious Life, in its very being, is the conscious qualities of enthusiasm, spontaneity, buoyancy, elasticity, agility, vigor, vitality, virility, and these qualities are ever in manifestation as the actual man and the only man. Does divine Mind ever operate consciously as the deflection of these qualities? Such a thought is unthinkable, unseeable, unfeelable.

Our textbook says, "Men and women of riper years and larger lessons ought to ripen into health and immortality, instead of lapsing into darkness or gloom. Immortal Mind feeds the body with supernal freshness and fairness, supplying it with beautiful images of thought and destroying the woes of sense which each day brings to a nearer tomb."

When our textbook makes these statements, it is Truth, or Mind, saying them to us, and since Truth, or Mind, says that we should ripen into health and immortality, then we can do it, and we should do it. But we shall not ripen into health and immortality by trying to ripen, or make immortal, the deflection. Actual man is already ripened and finished as to his health and his immortality, and we do not need to do anything to actual man. But we should turn from the deflection and find ourselves in oneness with the infinite, immortal qualities of God.

7. SUPPLY

Some years ago a Christian Science lecturer made this startling statement from the platform, "It is a sin to be poor." Shortly after this a prominent Christian Scientist said to me, "There is no sense in so much lack among Scientists, when they know what to do about the Science of supply." And again, another Christian Scientist whose experience and quality of thought was above the average, made this pointed declaration: "Insufficient supply is a disease, as much as insufficient health."

These statements challenged my orthodox way of thinking. Unconsciously, like many others, I was holding to the old belief that a deprivation of wealth often developed worthy traits of character. I was holding to the thought that poverty and lack were virtues, when in reality, poverty and lack are sin. I soon found that the average thought in regard to supply was very feeble thinking. Like myself, nearly all Christian Scientists were walking in or with the currents of mortal mind when it came to the demonstration of their supply.

Students, we as Christian Scientists are entering this new age fully aware that we cannot escape the results of our own thinking. If we think in or with the currents of mortal mind, we receive the results of such thinking; and when we think with our God-endowed dominion, we experience God's ever-present supply. We reap our harvest from the thinking which we maintain. Today, we are where our thinking has brought us, and no matter what our present environment is, we shall fall, remain stationary, or rise to new heights, according to the thoughts we maintain.

The whole world knows that supply is vital to the well-being of mankind. As Christian Scientists, we understand that fundamentally our supply already exists. We understand that the Science that demonstrates health, is the same Science that demonstrates supply. We are taught that every human heart can have its rightful need supplied, whether that need is "a child of promise," like Isaac, St. John, and Jesus, or the need of loaves and fishes, or the need of tax money.

We who understand something of Christian Science, believe that the Science of supply exists, is established, and is as workable as is the science of mathematics. When once we clearly understand that the character of supply is as mental as mathematics is mental, we shall have our supply at hand all the time. We do not go outside of our own mind to get the mathematical value we need, and we do not go outside of our own mind to get the supply that we need.

Jesus did not go anywhere to get the loaves and fishes. He turned at once to his own Mind for his needed supply. Jesus knew that loaves and fishes were purely mental; they were thought-forms, or forms of thought. He knew that each individual consciousness already included loaves and fishes, and all other good as well. Jesus proved in this demonstration that we already are the infinite supply that God is being.

Everything of which we have been conscious, and everything that we ever shall be conscious of, even now makes up our consciousness. There is nothing external to or apart from our consciousness. Our supply is purely mental, and consists of infinite, divine ideas in our consciousness. These divine ideas are perfect and established, and make up our individual consciousness throughout eternity.

Infinite good is the all of each of us, just as the qualities of the sun are the all of each individual ray of light. The father said to the prodigal — that is, the prodigal's own mind said to the prodigal — "Son, thou art ever with your own infinite Mind, and all that your own infinite Mind is, is you." To be one with our own Father, Mind, is to be Mind's presence — is to be the infinite good which appears to us as all things.

When we understand that our supply is purely mental and consists of ideas already within our own mind, we shall experience our supply of things without delay, without mental labor, and without the sweat of our brow. Whatever may be our supply tomorrow or next year, was our supply a thousand years ago. Our supply of infinite divine ideas has been inherent in divine Mind — our Mind — from the beginning. There is no time nor distance between supply and our own Mind that is being our supply. Whatever seems to be over there, as supply, is here in our own consciousness as an infinite divine idea.

Bicknell Young has said, "The time will come when Christian Scientists by the thousands will think with the profundity of the divine Mind, without processes, and will acquire the objects of their thinking without delay, and with the certainty of the divine Mind."

It does seem at times that the human being wants and needs many things. This is mortal mind's worst malpractice. In reality we are never in a state of need or want, because the infinite divine ideas in consciousness are already complete and established. This fact of our completeness forever excludes our needing or wanting anything. To want something keeps us from having it.

Since we already possess the infinitude of divine ideas in our consciousness, we cannot at the same time need or desire anything. When we finally overcome our ignorance of the Science of supply, we shall find ourselves in possession of all things. We shall find ourselves secure, abundantly supplied, and satisfied.

Many are saying at this time, As soon as the war is over, we shall have automobiles, and gasoline, and tires, and sugar, and many other things. But, students, why should we wait until the war is over? The five thousand could have been fed later in the day, but Jesus saw no need of waiting. Jesus knew that every one in that company of five thousand already possessed loaves and fishes, as well as all other divine ideas, that very instant, by way of reflection. Jesus understood that supply was mental and eternally present as divine ideas in consciousness. Like the science of mathematics, the Science of supply was a mental operation to Jesus, and by exercising this Science, the loaves and fishes were at hand.

In the textbook Mrs. Eddy admonishes us: "Establish the scientific sense of health, and you relieve the oppressed organ." And, students, we should likewise establish in our consciousness the scientific sense of supply, and in this way relieve the oppressed condition. And we should keep on establishing this scientific sense of supply until the various forms of lack are spiritually healed. When we recognize that lack is merely a false claim and never an entity, we no longer fear it; and the complete destruction of the claim quickly follows. Supply is purely mental; and when we displace the sense of lack with the true sense of supply, this sense of supply which we entertain will be manifest in our human experience.

Our heavenly Father is ever conscious of abundance; and by the law of divine reflection, we can individualize this consciousness of abundance. It is a present spiritual fact that we possess abundance, and nothing can interfere with our expression of it. Having once gained this consciousness of abundance, we can never lose it, for it is the scientific sense of supply. Wherever we go, we take it with us; and should everything that makes up our present human sense of supply be temporarily swept away, our scientific sense of supply still remains undisturbed and will manifest itself.

In *Unity of Good*, Mrs. Eddy tells us, "Jesus required neither cycles of time nor thought in order to mature fitness for perfection and its possibilities. He said that the kingdom of heaven is here, and is included in Mind; that while ye say, There are yet four months, and then cometh the harvest, I say, Look up, not down, for your fields are already white for the harvest; and gather the harvest by mental, not material processes."

8. BUSINESS

You may be thinking, and quite naturally so, What can she give us on business, other than a few academic statements which are mostly assumptions on her part? She has never run a business! But neither did Jesus ever run a shoe factory, a dry-goods store, a cannery, a grain elevator or a farm, yet he was the greatest businessman in the world.

The world will never know a greater business executive than Jesus. No red tape prevented him from making delivery of the loaves and fishes, the wine at the wedding feast, and the tax money, instantly. Jesus knew nothing about delay or future delivery. Jesus recognized omnipresent good at hand and the only thing at hand.

Since Jesus was always about his Father's business, what was Jesus' business? Jesus' business was to express or show forth to the world all the infinite actualities — all the conscious operations — of his Father, Mind. Everything of which he was conscious was to him an actuality — one with his Father, Mind. Everything, every actuality, was something for him to utilize and show forth and operate according to His will.

Every activity of the divine Mind is primarily a business activity, and is wholly mental. Humanly speaking, every activity of the divine Mind is for the purpose of supplying the specific wants and needs of mankind. There is nothing going on in the whole world but business activity. Business of every name and nature is infinite activity — infinite actualities of the divine Mind expressed humanly; and like Jesus the business of each one of us is to utilize, show forth, and be this activity and actuality of the divine Mind.

To Jesus, all business activities were evolved by the divine Mind, according to the divine will, and were governed by the divine Mind, even to the slightest detail. To Jesus, all business activities went on unceasingly and in divine order. Since divine Mind was infinite business, Jesus, being the full expression of divine Mind, expressed or functioned as infinite business.

Since we are not separate from God, our own Mind, we are not something separate from our business. All there is to us, is divine Mind expressed as business. Our very nature and being are dominion, possession, expression, evidence. We embody opportunity, capacity, ability. Since we express the infinitude of the divine Mind, then whenever a higher realization of business appears as our consciousness, there appears also the inevitable conscious evidence of a better business.

According to sense testimony, and especially in the light of actuality, there is entirely too much feeble thinking about business going on among Christian Scientists. We find it much easier to walk into or with the currents of mortal thought concerning our business, than to overthrow within ourselves this disastrous, feeble thinking that is purely mortal mind thinking.

We are the dominion that divine Mind is being, and we should see to it that divine Mind in its fulfillment operates as our business. The only way in which we can change business conditions is to change our own thinking. Our thinking and our business are identical. We change our business conditions within our own thought only — that is the only place we know anything about business. So much of the feeble thinking that is being indulged in by Christian Scientists should be "an offense" unto us. As Christian Scientists, we should be awake and inherit.

According to belief, or generally speaking, business is the expression of the mass thinking of human beings. The human being and his business are one. Business is the expression of the human being's thought. What we call business appears very human, very emotional. It appears to have heart and soul. It appears to live and die. According to belief, business is dependent entirely upon the human being who thinks it. Business is very sensitive to the good or bad thinking of the individual businessman.

Good or bad business germinates in our thinking. Bad business invariably results from bad thinking, from poor judgment, from mental fear, and especially from our own mental malpractice and mental persecution about our own individual business. Good business prevails with universal good thinking. Good scientific thinking within ourselves, about our own business, germinates security and provides us humanly with right and legitimate wants and needs.

Our highest sense of business, is that it will supply our legitimate wants and needs. So long as human beings remain civilized, and use their minds to think about the wants and needs of the people, there will be in evidence what we call business activity. At this moment, the United States is so concerned and so involved mentally in world events, that she is drifting away from the normal wants and needs of mankind. When a people become subnormal in their thinking, the business very quickly becomes subnormal. There has never been a time in all history when unity of thought among men is more vitally needed than it is today. There has never been a time when strong constructive thinking, from every human being who knows how to reflect true thought, is so much needed.

Divine Love does not give us things in the usual sense of the word give. We are already all that divine Love is being. The belief that divine Love gives what we desire is comforting, but it is purely a human view, and is only relatively true. The fact is that we cannot even have a desire. Before a desire can be uttered, we already possess that very thing.

God shows forth all that He is through His manifestation, man. Our business is to utilize and show forth to the world these infinite actualities of the divine Mind that are already ours by virtue of our oneness with the divine Mind. As our thinking becomes like divine Principle, or is the thinking that divine Principle is being, then this divine Principle within us, as us, evidences itself forth as infinite good or a good business.

Have you ever tried to hold your thought in oneness with the divine Principle that governs your business for three consecutive days? I wish each one of you would try it. It may seem arduous at first, but when you really start from the Father's house (the true consciousness about business), true consciousness will come out to meet you and will embrace you, and make a feast of good things for you — tangible things, things according to your highest comprehension of what they should be as business.

When working for our business, we do not think so much about ways and means of business, but we think of Principle — that is, we keep our thought active as divine Truth. We bring every human thought about business into subjection to divine Truth. This Truth, active in our consciousness, takes care of ways and means in our business. Our individual mind is the one Mind — the one Principle — and is already in conscious expression and operation as the so-called material ways and means. Like Jesus, our business is to recognize this fact of divine Principle, utilize it, and let it express itself.

We do not outline in business. We often feel that certain things in our business should occur in a certain way, which we have more or less outlined. But Principle, Truth, alone outlines its own activities and operations, and these go on eternally. When we think as Principle, or think as though we were Principle itself doing the thinking, then we have real demonstration in our business — demonstration that far exceeds our outlining.

But it is not by thinking only that we overcome human difficulties in business. We think the truth pertaining to our business, and then we must execute this truth. The thinking and the concrete evidence is a unit. Jesus always presented the concrete evidence, human or material, of Truth in all his demonstrations.

We might declare Principle, or Truth, all day; but if this Principle, or Truth, is not wrought out in concrete human or material evidence, we shall not get very far in our business. It is not enough just to say a lot of statements of Truth. We must declare the truth with full conviction that Truth is true, and then this truth must be wrought out in our business. In this way only does Truth become a law to our business.

It is our business to make our business pay, and we do this by strict adherence to divine Principle. So-called human business is really divine business appearing humanly. Then, because of its divine source, our human business should be better every day. Every Christian Scientist should be getting richer, not because we desire material riches, but because we are demonstrating infinity. And there is no limit to infinity.

Practically all business is carried on in order to have an income, and this is as it should be. And it is natural for us to look to our business for our income, rather than to look to infinite Mind. But we may be sure that our business will yield a better income, when we understand that our business is infinite Mind itself, expressed infinitely as our income. Our business is not a medium for our income, but our business *is* our income.

Mrs. Eddy has written the following article, entitled, "My Income":

> *My income is Life, and Love, and Truth. It is equal to all demands made upon it. This income is my inalienable possession derived from no earthly source, supplied through no material channels, dependent upon no personality or personal effort, not even my own, but coming to me direct from God. It is mine to receive, to possess, to use, but never to waste or hoard. It is to be received without fear, or doubt, shared without apprehension that all supply can fail. 'All things that the Father hath are mine.' These come to me and constitute my income unfailingly, abundantly, ample for any demand that can be made upon it.*

Businessmen often think that their business is regulated by the government, or by adverse circumstances over which they have no control. But in reality, business is governed by divine Principle alone. We include our business in our thought, and it depends upon the consciousness we entertain about it. *We are not in our business; our business is within us.* Business cannot think whether it will be good or bad, but is governed entirely either by our thought that is Principle or by our thought that is belief. There is nothing in outside circumstances that can interfere with our business.

Adverse circumstances — even the extreme circumstances of death and corruption — did not interfere with Jesus' business of showing forth the concrete evidence of ever-present Life and wholeness that was Lazarus. To Jesus, life was an actuality. It came from divine Mind. It was governed and controlled by divine Mind and was forever expressed by the life of Lazarus. Jesus knew that life was a fact of divine Principle; He made this fact active as his consciousness and the concrete evidence of life appeared.

Divine Principle governs our business absolutely and imperatively. We may find it difficult to demonstrate this fact instantaneously, but we shall experience fewer difficulties when we remember that divine Principle demonstrates its own facts. When we clear away false beliefs — the aggressive mental suggestions, the deflections of actualities — from our thinking, we shall find the spiritual facts of business at hand, in the same way that Jesus found the fact of life at hand. We should never permit our thinking to be regimented into or with the currents of mortal thought concerning business. Our thought should be kept in line with the facts of divine Principle, and these facts should be kept active as our consciousness.

Every businessman should understand his business to the slightest detail. He should manage his business according to the highest business principles. He should fit himself for leadership, and earnestly strive to improve the control of his business. When he has others in his employ, he should be able to instruct them in what they should do, and how they should do it, and then see that the work is properly done.

When a Christian Scientist brings himself and his employees and his activities in line with the facts of divine Principle, he has been doing much more than establishing right activity in his business. Such a Christian Scientist is helping to establish Church. He is giving proof that his business is Church, because it "rests upon and proceeds from divine Principle." Business, when correctly understood, is never material, but is divinely spiritual.

Whatever the nature of our business activity, we should always be practical. We should become skilled, practiced and experienced in our business. Jesus was practical, and he was always successful. What we need to make our business practical is Love and more Love. But there is nothing soft about Love. Love is as keen as steel. Love is Principle, and Principle demands of us that we discipline our thought, and use our God-bestowed dominion in our business.

Sometimes a Christian Scientist whose understanding is somewhat limited will say, "All is Love," and then let his business take care of itself the best it can. Through this mistaken sense of Love, his business is very apt to be lost. Just to say, "All is Love," without the concrete evidence of Love's presence, is not enough. Christian Scientists should be alert, intelligent, prompt, and utilize and show forth the concrete facts of Principle, Love, in their business.

In the business world today, we seem to come face to face with much personal propaganda, much selfishness and greed, dishonesty and lack of cooperation. All this is animal magnetism and mental malpractice; but as Christian Scientists, do we fear these beliefs of life and intelligence in matter — these deflections of actualities? Animal magnetism and mental malpractice are nothing claiming to be something, and Mrs. Eddy says, "Why should we stand aghast at nothingness?" We should not let these false suggestions in our business deceive us. We know where we contact them, and where to destroy them. Students, we control our business through the understanding that business is mental and spiritual and governed by divine Mind; or our business controls us through our belief that it is apart from us and is material and governed by many minds. We control our business with the truth we entertain, or our business controls us through the beliefs we entertain.

One of the first scientific principles that a Christian Scientist puts into practice in the business world is the fact that when he knows a thing humanly, there exists at hand its actuality. The Christian Scientist begins to understand, to have faith, and to demonstrate, that the actuality of his business is all there is to his business humanly. And he gives proof that not only his stomach and heart and lungs, but his stocks, his money, his office force, and his salesmen, are divine activities, although imperfectly seen by him. Actualities only are at hand. The human concept, like the mirage lake, does not add to the actuality, nor take from the actuality; there is present only divine actuality.

All there is to what we call stocks and bonds, to securities of all kinds, and to our business, is the divine actuality at hand. In their reality, these are something that divine Mind is consciously being. They are established and secure, and permanent in the compound idea man. The human concept of stocks and bonds, of securities, and of business, is that they are material, that they are separate from God and separate from our consciousness, that their value can fluctuate or that they can be lost altogether. What an untrue concept of actuality! What an untrue concept of God and His compound idea man!

It may be that we have experienced a sense of loss in our stocks or bonds or our business. But stocks or bonds or business, even in belief, have nothing to do with our sense of loss. This seeming sense of loss is formed wholly by mortal mind. Mortal mind has made the law that if we have stocks or bonds or business, that it is possible for us to have the sense of loss. But the stocks and bonds and business had nothing to do with forming it, and man had nothing to do with forming it. The sense of loss is wholly mortal mind sense. Nobody or nothing caused it. It is mesmerism — a deflection of an actuality.

We have all been on a train that was standing still when another train passed by, and we all had the sense that our train was moving. Now, the sense of moving was wholly within us. But mortal mind alone is the sense of moving. We did not have the sense of movement; neither we nor the train moved.

There is no more truth to our sense of loss than to our sense of movement. We handle any false sense as no sense, whether it is pain or disease or loss. We detach the pain or disease from the body; likewise, we detach the loss from the stocks and bonds, and from our business; and we understand that this false sense was not formed by our Mind — was not formed at all.

We meet the sense of loss when we understand that it is without cause, that it is wholly apart from ourselves, and wholly disconnected from stocks and bonds and business. We meet within ourselves the suggestion that there is a sense of loss, or that there ever has been a sense of loss. When we understand that a sense of loss is never our sense and is never a reality, then we shall see our stocks and bonds and our business in their actuality, established and unfailing in their perfection.

The only man there is — the real man — does not know a stock market with fluctuations. The real man knows actualities only. The only thing that represents God is God Himself. There are no values outside the infinity of God. Infinite good, by reflection, is possessed by each one of us, and if this infinite good appears to our consciousness as stocks and bonds, or business, then they must have the actuality or quality of actuality. They cannot fluctuate or be lost because they are actualities, even though imperfectly seen by us, and they can only unfold to us a higher good.

The seeming mortal mind that appears to be here, and says there is something that can be lost, is not here. There is no mortal mind. Business cannot be lost, because it is an actuality. If we seem to have experienced loss in the past, we can still prove that what seemed to be lost is still intact in its perfect completeness. And if we do not reproduce it in the form in which it seems to be lost, we shall find it in a higher form of good. How can this be true? It is true because our human concept is constantly rising higher — rising into reality. It is never too late to take up the sense of loss and dispose of it scientifically.

Another scientific principle that Jesus practiced in his business was the reciprocal law of being that governs the relationships of man. According to human sense, business involves many minds, many opinions, many degrees of education, etc. But in all these things Jesus practiced scientific relationship — a relationship that was mental and spiritual, and not personal relationship at all.

Relationship in business always "rests upon and proceeds from divine Principle." Divine Principle has infinite ways and means with which to supply the businessman. These ways and means are open, free and unobstructed. They operate as reciprocal laws of being that coordinate and are fitly joined together. What is apparent to human thought as one person or thing supplying the need of another person or thing, is the reciprocal law of being reflecting the wholeness of itself to each individual expression of itself. Students, we should more and more recognize and utilize this reciprocal law of being that is ever in operation in our behalf, and in behalf of those with whom we deal.

These deeper things of Mind are not always easy to comprehend, but they will unfold to those who have eyes to see, and ears to hear. There are some here today who will go along in the usual grooves of mortal thought for another season, but there are many here who will rise to heights before unknown.

9. MONEY

There is, perhaps, no other one thing of which we are conscious, and which gives us so much concern, as money. This is because we have been educated to believe that our wants and needs can be supplied only if we have money. But in our study of Christian Science, we understand that we have all things — money included — because divine Mind expresses all things, all actualities, as man. It is as much a fact that we have money, as it is a fact that we have food, or clothing, or health, or heart, or hand, or air to breathe.

When correctly understood, money is one of Mind's divine ideas. Incorrectly considered, money is the false human concept of a divine idea. In its divine actuality, money is a very high idea in its expression of substance. Hence, in our human expression of substance, the desire to have money seems greater than all other desires. When we lose the material sense of money, and understand it as divine idea in oneness with divine Mind, then we shall find it always present and established in our consciousness.

Since money is an infinite idea in the compound idea man, it is inevitable that each and every individual must have money in some form, and must have it all the time. Our textbook tells us that man "is the compound idea of God, including all right ideas." Then we already include the right idea of money. When we clearly understand that money is a divine idea, and that we include this divine idea in consciousness, then the world's false sense of money as material, and as separate from divine Mind, and as separate from man, will not touch us; and humanly we shall have all the money we need all the time.

We, as Christian Scientists, should maintain a fixed scientific mental position in regard to money. As long as it seems necessary to have money humanly, we should be persistent in our thinking that we always have money in its actuality. When once we have established the fact that money in its actuality is a divine idea in consciousness, and that we already include it, and include it eternally, then we shall have its corresponding identity humanly. When Jesus needed the tax money, he had it because he knew that he already possessed the actuality or the divine fact of money eternally. Jesus dealt with actualities or facts only, and he had the corresponding identity instantly at hand, humanly or materially.

Mrs. Eddy says in *Miscellany*, "Till Christian Scientists give all their time to spiritual things, live without eating, and obtain their money from a fish's mouth, they must earn it in order to help mankind with it." Nevertheless Mrs. Eddy, herself, proved that money was ever a divine idea in consciousness. It is recorded that for many mornings when her need was very great, she found a dollar bill inside her door, and it was placed there by no human hand. And today we shall have our money readily, and the earning of it made easier, when we clearly understand that both the money and the earning of it, are the divine Mind expressed humanly. Students, let us awake and inherit!

10. I AM

It was not until Mary Baker Eddy gave us *Science and Health with Key to the Scriptures* that we were able to understand the statement, I AM THAT I AM. The unillumined thought has no apprehension of the I, or Ego, other than the personal I.

Mrs. Eddy uses the term I AM as a synonym for God, and defines I AM as, "God; incorporeal and eternal Mind; divine Principle; the only Ego." She says God is "the forever I AM. . . than which there is naught else." She says God is "the ever-present I AM, filling all space."

When we fully understand the term I AM, it does away with our belief of God as a person, and our belief in a personal I. We often hear such expressions as "I am ill," or "I am tired," or "I am poor," or "I am afraid" — all from the personal-I standpoint.

The one eternal I AM, governing all existence, forever excludes the possibility of there being a personal-I self, and it excludes all sin and suffering and death, which results from the belief in a personal-I self. Jesus beheld the perfect man; that is, within his own consciousness he beheld an individual expression of God, the great I AM. But those who accompanied Jesus beheld within their consciousness this expression of the great I AM in reversion. They saw the perfect man as personal, and as entirely separate and apart from God.

We are so prone to think of ourselves and others as good personal human beings, or as good spiritually-minded personalities, who are trying to find the light of Truth. And while this is a commendable concept, it is a limited human concept. When correctly understood, we stand for something far greater than just good human beings or good personalities. In our actuality, we are radiant spiritual characters making up the Christ. The I AM is self-revealing, and is forever revealed to Himself as all individual men and women — the Christ. When correctly estimated, each one of us is the revealed Christ.

Where is our true vision? Of what avail is it for us to declare and affirm that God — the great I AM — is the only power, the only Life, the only presence, the one infinite being, if we go right on seeing and believing that we ourselves, and every man and woman is a personality — each with a life of his own, who thinks and acts according to a will of his own? Where is our true vision?

Our thought that I am this, I am that, I do this, I do that, I think this, I think that, is also on our lips many, many times each day, and always from a personal-I standpoint. But divine Science and our own good vision indicate that we should, at least as frequently, insist upon the fact that we are I AM in manifestation. The belief that we are a personal-I is the fundamental evil, and this false I is to be seen and dealt with as a deflection of the one and only I — the great I AM. As Christian Scientists, we should yield this sense of personality, and claim the real I AM THAT I AM as the All and Only. All the troubles of the human race are traced directly or indirectly to a false material sense of the one divine I AM. And it is by acknowledging and accepting the one divine I AM as the only I, that we learn to surrender our false beliefs of sin, sickness, lack and death, which are all incidental to the so-called personal-I.

In all her writings, Mrs. Eddy has taken particular pains to make clear and definite that the only I AM is never expressed by the finite, material, mortal or personal. The I AM THAT I AM does not mean the mortal and material; it does not mean personal perfection; it does not mean anything that is limited or finite. The great I AM of all being is not restricted, neither is it restrictive. I AM does not know fear, and knowing no fear is to be infinitely individual and infinitely universal.

At this very instant, if we were conscious of ourselves as the I AM THAT I AM, what would we be thinking? As the conscious identity or manifestation of I AM, we would be thinking (and our thinking would be our being it), I AM infinite, eternal Mind, immaculate, immortal. I exist in and of myself. I forever know my own ideas. I know ALL. I am harmonious, joyful, free. I AM THAT I AM understood, means the one intelligence —the intelligence that we are now; the one being — the being that we are now; the one Life — the life we are now; the one divine Principle from which we are never diverted nor subverted.

Right where we think, right where we dwell, right where our consciousness says "I" — right there is I AM THAT I AM. What the personal sense seems to know humanly, is not we personally knowing something apart from the divine Mind. It is divine Mind — the only I AM — consciously being Himself as real man. It is never we, as person, saying, God is the only power, the only Life, the only presence. It is always the I AM, and never the personal-I that declares power and Life and presence, and is being it. This event that is taking place here today — our association — is a legitimate event, and whatever is true about this event is God — the I AM — being it. If we take a drive this evening, or go to our business next Monday morning, there is no other than the great I AM being these events. The truth or fact to these events, and to all events, is the I AM THAT I AM.

The divine I AM finds expression in everything that He thinks; He finds expression in all that He knows and does; the divine I AM is the basis of all true action and achievement. There is but one I AM, and this I AM speaks and it is done. When we clearly understand that the only I AM is God, and that we are the evidence or conscious identity of this self-existent God, and when we understand that there has never been a time when this self-existent I AM could get along without what He is — what man is — then we are not afraid to say I AM. We know that the only thing that is saying I AM, is our infinite divine Mind. It is our own infinite consciousness that is saying I AM, and not us personally. When we say I AM, we are really finding our own divine actuality.

Man, the man we are right now, is the evidence or conscious identity of this great I AM. I AM(meaning God) and THAT I AM (meaning man) is in unity, in oneness. We are the expression, the manifestation, the conscious identity of the I AM, God. I AM infinity, is man in effect as infinity.

I AM is the only Mind, knowing all. And in the measure that we — the manifestation of the all-knowing Mind — show forth scientific thinking, without selfishness, without greed, without fear, without doubt, without any sense of will or domination — just the serene thought that the divine Mind is being our Mind — in the measure that we do this, it is the divine Mind, the I AM, doing our thinking. It is this I THAT I AM that heals the sick and the sinner, that reduces every difficulty in our business or daily affairs to its nothingness, and brings success and achievement.

The term I AM is a most important expression in the unfoldment of Christian Science to the individual consciousness. Without it we are apt to think of God or the "I" as being afar off, when right here is the place that the "I" possesseth. A great sense of freedom and dominion comes to us when we realize that the I AM's knowledge of Himself is our individual self. I AM THAT I AM— we should say it, and think it, and be it, all the time. We should say and know I AM THAT I AM from the standpoint of the one divine Mind as being All. It is most unscientific to say it from the standpoint of the personal-I; and to make the scientific statement, I AM THAT I AM, to the unprepared thought is not the way of wisdom.

Moses was appointed to deliver the children of Israel from bondage — that is, from all mental darkness, doubt and fear. Moses demurred, saying, "Who am I that I should bring the children of Israel out of Egypt?" Moses sensed that it would take a greater power than he, as a personal I, to do this mighty task. Then God or true consciousness said to Moses, I AM THAT I AM. In this tremendous statement of absolute supremacy, Moses recognized that it is the ever-present I AM — the Christ within — and not a personal I, that delivers mankind from all material bondage.

To affirm from the personal standpoint that I am sick, I am afraid, I am discouraged, I am tired, I am angry, I am poor, or any other erroneous assertions that we are so prone to make regarding our personal-I self, is merely forging another link in our chain of bondage. Our business is to be the truth about ourselves — to be the limitless good, the opportunity, the ability, the possessions, the capacity, that God, the great I AM, is expressing as His manifestation, man. Our heritage is dominion and perfection and power, because the scientific fact is that *now* we are the conscious identity of the great I AM.

Mrs. Eddy has beautifully portrayed in *Science and Health* the limitless horizon of our individual being as the reflection of Spirit — the great I AM. We read: "I am Spirit. Man, whose senses are spiritual, is my likeness. He reflects the infinite understanding, for I am Infinity. The beauty of holiness, the perfection of being, imperishable glory, — all are Mine, for I am God. I give immortality to man, for I am Truth. I include and impart all bliss, for I am Love. I give life, without beginning and without end, for I am Life. I am supreme and give all, for I am Mind. I am the substance of all, because I AM THAT I AM."

ABOUT THE AUTHOR: Martha Wilcox was a prominent teacher during the years when the Christian Science organization was at its peak of prosperity. She grew up on a farm in Kansas, under the influence of a religious family life. She studied privately for a Teacher's Certificate and became a teacher in the local schools. Before finding Christian Science, she was an active member of the Methodist Church. It was through a series of events, in which she sought medical aid for her ailing husband, that she was presented in 1902 with a copy of *Science and Health*. As she studied and pondered this book, she was healed of a physical problem of long-standing. While her husband was not interested in Christian Science, she definitely was.

Within the next six years, she had Primary class instruction, became an active member of a branch church in Kansas City, Missouri, and managed to devote much of her time to the healing work, in addition to caring for her family. In 1908 she received a call from The Mother Church in Boston asking her to serve Mrs. Eddy at her home in Chestnut Hill, Massachusetts.

In Mrs. Wilcox's first interview with Mrs. Eddy, it was impressed upon her that everything in one's experience is subjective or mental. Mrs. Wilcox writes of this interview: "[Mrs. Eddy], no doubt, realized that at my stage of growth, I thought of creation — that is, all things — as separated into two groups, one group spiritual and the other group material. But during this lesson I caught my first glimpse of the fact that all right, useful things — which I had been calling 'the unrighteous mammon' — were mental and represented spiritual ideas. She showed me that unless I were faithful and orderly with the objects of sense that made up my present mode of consciousness, there would never be revealed to me the 'true riches,' or the progressively higher revealments of substance and things."

Mrs. Wilcox later wrote: "I well remember when for the first time I understood that everything of which I am conscious is thought, and never external to or separate from what I call my mind, and that which I call my mind is not always seeing things as they actually are."

In 1910, Mrs. Wilcox was recommended by Mrs. Eddy for Normal Class instruction, with Bicknell Young as teacher. This was the beginning of a long and successful career for Mrs. Wilcox as a practitioner and teacher. In 1911, she taught her first class. Until her passing in 1948, she was dedicated to serving the Christian Science movement, and became one of the most respected teachers in the Field. She was the author of many profound papers on Christian Science, mainly papers given each year to her association of students.

Mrs. Wilcox's two years with Mrs. Eddy equipped her to understand so well the subjective nature of all things. She explains how to shift the focal point of thought from the objective world of people, things, happenings, to the subjective world of intuitions, thoughts, ideas. Although she stresses the mental cause of disease and discord, she goes beyond an analysis of the human mind and explains how to relate to God subjectively through prayer; how to develop an understanding of Him that spiritualizes consciousness and heals, how to transcend the false material view of creation and find the spiritual view.

At the time that Mrs. Wilcox wrote these addresses, the Church organization would not permit the publication or circulation of such papers. But Mrs. Wilcox did share them privately with students, and they were handed down over the years to the present time. In giving these papers to her students, it is possible that Mrs. Wilcox hoped they would someday go forth to bless the world, for surely she must have been aware of their timeless message.

For further information regarding Christian Science:
Write: The Bookmark
        Post Office Box 801143
        Santa Clarita, CA 91380
Call: 1-800-220-7767
Visit our website: www. thebookmark.com